Praise for *The Supply Chain Revolution*

Successful companies in every industrial sector have long recognized that competitive advantage comes not just from the products or services that they offer but from the supply chains that support them. In this easy-to-read and insightful book, the author explores the opportunities that exist for improving profitability through supply chain excellence and provides practical guidance on how to achieve that goal.

—Martin Christopher, Emeritus Professor of Marketing & Logistics, Cranfield School of Management, UK

The Ideal Supply Chain Primer for the Time-Pressed CEO or Government Executive
In clear, concise language Suman Sarkar demystifies the complexities of supply chain management. The key to his process is simplification. In a world of business books full of buzzwords and unnecessary complications, this is a refreshing approach. Sarkar breaks supply chain management into its component pieces and succinctly lays out the relationships. If you are getting foggy, conflicting advice from staff and suppliers, as I frequently did in a career managing large organizations, you will find this short read welcome clarification.

—Richard Connelly, Hall of Fame, Former Budget Leader, Energy Director, Defense Logistics Agency, Department of Defense, USA

Wonderful Book for Supply Chain and Business Leaders
Suman has written a wonderful book for supply chain and business leaders. He has presented examples that tell the story of the fundamentals in a memorable way. It demonstrates the value of supply chain in delivering bursts results. I highly recommend him to anyone leading a supply chain.

—Mary Anne Gale, Retired VP of Supply Chain, Procter & Gamble

Solid Advice for Busy Leaders
In this quick-read, rich with examples, Suman describes the what and why of supply chain debottlenecking, providing timeless, tried and true advice on how to simplify and streamline supply chains in clear and easily understood language. Suman ends with the all important business imperative of supply chains providing a competitive edge to firms doing this well. Especially relevant in this digital age of online shopping and rapid product innovation.

—Isabelle Konstantinov, Former Product Supply Associate Director, Procter & Gamble

THE
SUPPLY
CHAIN
REVOLUTION

INNOVATIVE SOURCING AND LOGISTICS
FOR A FIERCELY COMPETITIVE WORLD

SUMAN SARKAR

HarperCollins
Leadership

AN IMPRINT OF HarperCollins

The Supply Chain Revolution

© 2017 Suman Sarkar

Published by HarperCollins Leadership, an imprint of HarperCollins Focus LLC.

Any internet addresses, phone numbers, or company or product information printed in this book are offered as a resource and are not intended in any way to be or to imply an endorsement by HarperCollins Leadership, nor does HarperCollins Leadership vouch for the existence, content, or services of these sites, phone numbers, companies, or products beyond the life of this book.

Bulk discounts available. For details visit:
www.harpercollinsleadership.com/bulkquotes
Email: customercare@harpercollins.com

ISBN 978-0-8144-3878-7 (HC)
ISBN 978-1-4002-4266-5 (paperback)

This book is dedicated to Sahana Rhea Sarkar and Niharika Ramdev for their love, encouragement, and support.

ACKNOWLEDGMENTS

THE CONCEPTS IN THE BOOK WERE developed for my clients. They trusted me with their resources and allowed me to experiment and develop the ideas that are shared in the book. I would like to acknowledge my profound respect for my clients and their teams.

Two people made the book more readable—Charles Wallace and Alan Farnham. Charles was the developmental editor and helped with structuring the content. He is an award-winning writer who excels at translating complex concepts into easy-to-understand prose. His critique of each chapter was enormously valuable, as he was able to point out where the logic did not flow and how to make technical concepts simple to follow. Alan helped in the writing of this book. He made it accessible to a broader audience by making the style less technical.

Several people reviewed each chapter for its content—Niharika Ramdev, Bill Shannon, Randy Hopkins, and Isabelle Konstantinov. Their industry knowledge, expert understanding of the subjects, and thoughtful critique helped to ensure that the content was accurate and of value to business readers.

A special thanks to Richard Connelly, who patiently reviewed the grammar in each chapter. His understanding of the subject and mastery of the language helped make the book more readable.

Also, thanks are due to two marketing experts—Abigail Fisher and Bob Heyman. Abigail is a social media marketing specialist who pushed me to develop a stronger social media presence. Bob is a digital marketing expert who helped me think through how to use social media for selling books. Their input on how to best market the book has been invaluable.

Finally, I would like to thank Michael Snell, agent, and Tim Burgard, editor at AMACOM, for trusting and believing in this author.

ACKNOWLEDGMENTS

It is difficult for a first-time author to get an agent and a publisher. Without Michael's guidance and support, this book would not have been widely distributed. Tim provided great suggestions on getting the book ready for publication.

CONTENTS

PART 1

INCREASE REVENUE WITH HELP FROM SUPPLY CHAIN AND SOURCING

CONTENTS

PART 2

REDUCE BUSINESS RISK THROUGH EFFICIENT OPERATIONS

CONTENTS

PART 3

IMPROVE PROFITABILITY FROM AREAS THAT ARE CURRENTLY OUT OF SCOPE FOR SOURCING ORGANIZATIONS

CONTENTS

PART4

DRIVE BUSINESS EXCELLENCE WITH HELP FROM SOURCING

THE
SUPPLY
CHAIN
REVOLUTION

INTRODUCTION

STEVE JOBS AND SUPPLY CHAIN

Steve Jobs, after he returned to Apple in 1997, set himself three goals to turn around the then-struggling company: Improve Apple's product pipeline, improve its marketing, and transform its supply chain.

Its supply chain! Why would Jobs—surely one of the century's most visionary leaders—apply himself to something so mundane?

CEOs hardly ever think about supply chain, regarding them as having about the same amount of sex appeal as broccoli. (They only view one subject as being still less sexy: sourcing, the other subject of this book.)

Jobs cared about supply chains because he knew the price Apple was paying for having one that was so shoddy and slipshod. He was able to imagine the competitive advantage the company would reap by transforming it into something better.

At the time, the company had on hand two to three months of supplier inventory and another two to three months of finished goods, forcing Apple to anticipate consumer wants four to six months ahead. Jobs decided that even he was not smart enough to do that. He deputized Tim Cook to revamp the system.

Cook reduced inventory from months to days. He closed factories and warehouses, using contract manufacturers instead. He made long-term deals with suppliers to guarantee Apple's supply of flash memory and other key components. He identified and removed bottlenecks in the supply chain. Because of his reforms, Apple became super fast at new product development and getting new products into the eager hands of consumers. As sales spiraled up, Jobs's focus on Apple's supply chain was vindicated.

Apple's approach to fixing the supply chain was a conventional one. They took the first step in fixing the supply chain so it was not a roadblock to the company's success. The field of supply chain has expanded into new areas that are revolutionizing business. It is now able to help businesses drive revenue, manage corporate risk, drive excellence, and continue to reduce costs.

NEED FOR SUPPLY CHAIN REVOLUTION

Despite examples such as this, most CEOs continue to ignore supply chain management and sourcing. One result, not surprisingly, is that the state of the art in these two fields has not changed much in 20 years.

In fact, today's practices are not much different from what they were in 1945 when war forced the then-modern discipline of chain management into being.

Simply put, a supply chain exists to take material from suppliers, move it through manufacturing, and then distribute it to customers or end users. In WWII, the end users were the army and the navy, which had to be supplied across multiple geographies through different transportation modes (land, sea, and air).

Just as well-functioning supply chains helped lead the United States to victory in WWII, so too did bottleneck or otherwise poorly functioning chains lead to defeat. It is no exaggeration to say that Hitler's setbacks at Stalingrad and in North Africa were in part the results of breakdowns in supply.

For decades after WWII, the military approach to supply chain management and sourcing served private industry perfectly well. Now, however, it does not. Across a wide spectrum of industries, once-potent companies are in trouble: Walmart, IBM, Procter & Gamble (P&G), Pfizer, HP. The business model of these companies is static, relying primarily on product differentiation and global expansion. As product differentiation and market expansion opportunities continue to be reduced, they are finding themselves at a competitive disadvantage. This problem cannot be addressed by spending more money on advertising or buying other businesses. It is in operational areas such as supply chain and sourcing that a competitive edge can be found.

So the bad news is that many famous business names now find themselves standing on a burning platform. The good news? The need for change can no longer be ignored.

We are entering a time of testing for business leaders: Those who can evolve will survive; those who can't won't. In an era when management will need to exploit every competitive advantage it can find, leaders who continue to think of supply chains and sourcing only in terms of cost reduction will be at a serious disadvantage. Success will come to leaders who learn to see them as potential drivers of revenue growth, innovation, and risk reduction.

The contrast could not be more clear between companies that have turned sourcing and supply chains into competitive weapons and those that have not.

ZARA'S SUPPLY CHAIN ADVANTAGE

At a time when many major retailers are closing stores and seeing profits fade—Macy's, Best Buy, Radio Shack, the Gap, Nordstrom, and Sears, to name but a few—evolutionary retailer Zara—with 6,777 stores in 88 countries—is thriving.

Compare Zara to, say, the Gap: By some estimates, it takes the Gap 9 to 12 months to get a new clothing design into its stores. Imagine trying to predict fashion trends far in advance, then having to procure the fabric and do the manufacturing. Zara estimates it needs only 10 to 15 days—a feat it credits to having a highly responsive, demand-driven supply chain.

Zara defies conventional wisdom about how supply chain should be run. It keeps almost half of its production in-house, leaves room for extra capacity, and manufactures and distributes products in small batches. The company manages design, warehousing, distribution, and logistics functions in-house. Zara offers a large variety of the latest designs quickly and in limited quantities, which allows them to command a higher fraction of the full retail ticket price (an estimated 85%) compared to the industry average (60% to 70%).

Its supply chain—that boring thing most CEOs cannot be bothered to think about—makes Zara the most valued company in the retail space with a market cap of $90 billion. Its founder, Amancio Ortega, is now the richest man in Europe. (For a moment in 2015, he was the richest man in the world, eclipsing Bill Gates.) Ortega's view on clothes? They are perishable commodities like fruit: People change styles frequently, depending on their whim or some fashion trend. Accordingly, Ortega designed his supply chain to allow Zara to get a new design to customers in as little as a week or two.

Let's now turn to sourcing.

TJX'S SOURCING ADVANTAGE

The TJX Companies, with a market valuation of close to $50 billion, owns brands including T.J. Maxx, Marshalls, and Home Goods. Its shareholders have benefited from 18 consecutive years of earnings-per-share growth. In its nearly four-decade history, it has had only one year of negative same-store sales. Sourcing, that other boring area, makes TJX a company other big retailers envy.

Bernard Cammarata, who founded TJX in 1976, uses a unique approach to sourcing: TJX buys its products from major brands at a discount and then sells them in its stores. What's available in the store last week may not be available this week. It is always a treasure hunt. This has created a loyal group of customers who keep coming back to see what's new. TJX University trains the company's buyers in the art of deal making. They are empowered to make millions of dollars in deals that in other companies would require approval from top management. They have turned traditional retail sourcing on its head and have thereby created value.

Examples of other companies that have achieved equally impressive results will be found later in this book. In every case, management possessed two virtues: first, the imagination to see that supply chain and sourcing, if managed right, could deliver greater benefits than the cost savings traditionally expected of them; and second, the courage to enact change.

ABOUT THE AUTHOR'S WORK

I personally have seen the results of these experiments: new supply and sourcing designs that drive revenue, increase innovation, promote excellence, and reduce risk.

For the past 20 years, I have consulted with leading U.S., European, and Asian corporations, first at A.T. Kearney, and then, starting eight years ago, at my own firm. I have worked with leading companies in high tech, retail, pharma, financial services, and telecom, plus the Department of Defense and other federal agencies on smaller projects. We are talking about the largest biotech company, the leading hedge fund, the largest facilities management provider, and the leading mul-tibrand retailer, just to name a few.

I pride myself on the ability to deliver long-lasting business results, particularly for companies with a strong culture, where standard ap-proaches may not work. Some of my past engagements have given me a close-up view of the challenges faced by sourcing and supply chain leaders. These professionals have impressed me as being capable of doing far more than is expected of them in their traditionally limited roles. Companies can use them to win markets and to drive amazing business results. It is a disservice to think of them as capable only of cutting costs.

The transition from old ways to new ways of thinking is never easy for individuals or for organizations. Yet it can be done. And it must be done if companies are to create new weapons of advantage.

THE BOOK

I explain in detail how companies of all shapes and sizes are unboxing their supply chains and sourcing, so as to achieve greater business value. Business value can be in the form of increased revenue, lower business risk, improved profitability, and achievement of excellence.

- **PART 1**—Increase Revenue with Help from Supply Chain and Sourcing

    Chapter 1—Drive Customer Satisfaction—Through Excellent Service: As product differentiation shrinks, some companies try to offer higher levels of service to win customers. There is a cost attached to that. Supply chain organizations can drive customer satisfaction and increase profitability by balancing service and cost through segmentation and incentives.

    Chapter 2—Boost Revenue with Supply Chain: Supply chain can increase revenue by enabling customization or personalization, globalization, and improving responsiveness to demand. It plays a key role in successfully bringing innovation to market and then supporting rapid growth.

    Chapter 3—Amplify Alliance Performance with Sourcing: Alliances are becoming critical for business success. A sourcing organization with expertise in managing supply relationships can improve alliance success.

- **PART 2**—Reduce Business Risk Through Efficient Operations

    Chapter 4—Debottleneck the Supply Chain and Reduce Risk: After years of neglect, supply chains in many organizations are unable to deliver products and services. They have become high-risk areas that need to be addressed in a systematic way before they can contribute to bigger objectives. Simplification is key to debottleneck supply chain processes.

Chapter 5—Increase Retail Success by Managing Store Investment: Sourcing can help ensure that strategic investments are executed in a commonsense fashion. For example, retailers spend millions of dollars each year on opening new stores and remodeling old ones. A store's ability to remain profitable in times of changing consumer demand depends on its overhead costs. Sourcing can reduce costs by engaging general contractors and trades in new and different ways.

Part 3—Improve Profitability from Areas That Are Currently Out of Scope for Sourcing Organizations

Chapter 6—Enhance Marketing Efficiency: Digital media have revolutionized marketing. Sourcing teams can use analytical tools to help make marketing campaigns, including digital, more efficient; they can help negotiate more favorable deals with marketing suppliers. Result: an increase in marketing return on investment (ROI).

Chapter 7—Smart Real Estate Outsourcing: Companies have outsourced portions of their business, such as information technology (IT), payroll, facilities management, and others, with the hope of improving employee service and reducing cost. Most outsourcing arrangements have failed to deliver on this promise. Sourcing organizations can help leaders identify better ways to benefit from relationships with suppliers, by using the latest analytic tools or by revising outsourcing agreements.

PART 4—Drive Business Excellence with Help from Sourcing

Chapter 8—Source Excellence: With more than half the work at any company now being performed by outside suppliers, management cannot hope to achieve excellence by ignoring sourcing. Sourcing teams need to play an earlier, deeper role in helping management define what kind of excellence is being sought, to find the best supplier and negotiate the right terms.

CHANGE MANAGEMENT

In terms of supply chain and sourcing, for organizations to become effective requires change from leadership, R&D, sales and marketing, and other functional departments. In my consulting experience, I have found that functional organizations have great reluctance to take input from supply chain and sourcing into account. They feel that they have the required expertise, and they are not sure if supply chain and sourcing incentives are aligned with their best interests.

It is true that supply chain and sourcing folks are not experts in functional areas—nor should they be expected to be. Function-specific knowledge should come from the functional folks. Nonetheless, supply chain and sourcing teams can help these organizations find new solutions to their problems and can negotiate deals on their behalf.

At the same time, supply chain and sourcing teams have to step out of their comfort zone—something easier said than done.

Most supply chain and sourcing organizations are comfortable with traditional roles, as they know the expectations they must meet and understand what it takes to meet them. Many organizations call themselves "world class" (which implies that they do not need to change and cannot contribute further). Leaders of these organizations ask, "Why fix something that isn't broken?"

While forcing change always risks pushback, the fact is that if companies do not attempt change, some competitor that is more determined and aggressive will break open the constraints and reap the benefits.

I am writing about supply chain management and sourcing because they are my passions. I understand the power of creativity that will be unleashed if businesses can harness the talent they already have in-house.

Clearly, leadership's lack of appetite for change is one of the greatest obstacles to improving today's generally poor state of supply chain practice. But there is nothing to be afraid of. Change can be managed. Leadership starts with identifying the root causes of bottlenecks and other shortcomings, then identifying the best fixes.

A large change program can take years to implement and can require a CEO's constant championing. Will your CEO and your organization step up to the challenge? I hope so. The payoff for wrestling with these "boring" subjects is simply too great to ignore.

We will start the book with an area that is traditionally thought to be out of scope for the supply chain organization: customer satisfaction. It's an area that can be revolutionized, and the following chapter provides a taste of how companies can improve customer service with the help of supply chain.

INCREASE REVENUE WITH HELP FROM SUPPLY CHAIN AND SOURCING

1

DRIVE CUSTOMER SATISFACTION — THROUGH EXCELLENT SERVICE

1

BENEFITING FROM EXCELLENT SERVICE

What do companies such as Amazon, Chick-fil-A, Apple, Marriott, Starbucks, and American Express have in common? They are all known for excellent customer service. Customers tend to be loyal to businesses that have great customer service, and many are willing to provide referrals to their friends, family, and colleagues. Consumers will blindly purchase from these companies despite the fact that some of their prices are higher than the competition's. It is the belief that if the customers are not happy with the product or service, the company will do everything it can to rectify the problem quickly; customers will not have to wait in line for an hour to get the problem fixed. Customer service is not only important for consumer-oriented businesses but also for businesses that service other large corporations. Companies embrace customer service as a way to stand out from the competition when product differentiation is low or customers are fickle.

Most people associate customer service with the interaction that takes place between a company and its customers, and not so much with supply chain. However, a company's ability to provide excellent customer service depends to a large extent on its operations—its ability to deliver a product or service quickly and as promised, or to replace or return a defective product quickly. You would not be happy to receive a fax machine from an online retailer when you ordered a printer, and then have to wait for four weeks to get the product replaced, despite the polite apologies of the customer service agent. You may forgive the error the first time but would be unlikely to order from the store again if it happened repeatedly.

For happy customers, consistency and quality of product or service delivery are important, and supply chain plays a critical role in making that happen. To be known for service, a company should have intimate knowledge of customer needs, develop service models that are difficult for the competition to match, and then find a way to get customers to pay for the better service. Involving the supply chain organization up front can help identify different service models that can be offered to the customer. The supply chain team can estimate the costs and effort associated with each. The sales team can then negotiate the price with the customer in a business-to-business situation.

Customer service is a team effort. It's important that frontline colleagues are supported by a well-oiled machine that can meet or exceed customer expectations.

AMAZON'S CUSTOMER SERVICE ADVANTAGE

When Jeff Bezos founded Amazon in 1994, he vowed to become obsessed about delivering excellent customer service. The success of Amazon was mainly due to Bezos's focus on meeting customer needs in unique ways that were difficult to replicate by competitors. Amazon has relied on and invested heavily in its supply chain capabilities to support customer needs.

Amazon has received both good and bad press, but one thing everyone agrees with is that Bezos's company has an outstanding customer service record. *USA Today*[1] reported in 2015 that "for the sixth consecutive year, Amazon.com has topped the customer service Hall of Fame. Less than 2% of survey respondents reported a poor experience, and 59.4% reported excellent customer service, by far the highest percentage among all companies reviewed."

Amazon's superior customer service is no accident; it comes from Bezos's personal commitment. A few quotes from him will help you understand his philosophy:[2]

- ▪ "We're not competitor obsessed, we're customer obsessed. We start with what the customer needs, and we work backwards."
- ▪ "Focusing on the customer makes a company more resilient." Bezos famously brings an empty chair to meetings to represent the most important person in the room—"the customer."
- ▪ "If you make customers unhappy in the physical world, they might each tell six friends. If you make customers unhappy on the Internet, they can each tell 6,000."

Bezos makes himself personally accessible to customers. He is known to forward customer complaints to the appropriate person in the company, adding a "?" in his email in order to ensure a prompt response and resolution to the problem. It is hard to compete with a company that has such outstanding customer service. Even Walmart is struggling against Amazon's onslaught.

Another example of Bezos's unique focus on customer service is his concept and implementation of Amazon Prime,[3] the company's breakthrough promise to deliver packages within two days. It's a service model that competitors find difficult to replicate. A decade ago, most packages took a week or more to get from door to door. Two-day shipment was so expensive that customers often preferred to visit a local Walmart or Target store if they needed something quickly.

Amazon's ability to provide two-day delivery derives from a focus on its supply chain, which reduces reliance on expensive UPS and FedEx services. It has an unparalleled distribution network and continues to improve it every day. Amazon is now investing in robots in its distribution centers to handle peak volume, expanding its truck and air fleet, and even tinkering with new ideas such as delivery by drones. Amazon is also expanding the concept of same-day delivery in many cities as well as toying with the idea of Uber-type services for delivery of packages. To make last-mile deliveries cost-effective, Amazon is opening warehouses near the major cities. As of 2016, Amazon is estimated to have 180 warehouses and can now deliver packages with in-house resources in 30 major metropolitan areas.[4]

Though Prime has increased shipping cost, it has also proved another important point for Amazon: Customers are willing to pay for better, faster service. Amazon has raised the Prime membership fee from $79 to $99 to pay for increased shipment cost, with minimal customer pushback—and membership continues to grow.

Bezos has upended the traditional belief that increased customer service comes with an increased cost. He has shown that customer service can be improved while remaining economical and, more importantly, has convinced customers to pay for expanded services.

BEST BUY'S CHALLENGES WITH CUSTOMER SERVICE

Let's look at another example: Best Buy. In 1966, Richard M. Schulze and a business partner opened Sound of Music, an electronics store specializing in stereos, in St. Paul, Minnesota. They renamed the store Best Buy in 1983 to reflect their marketing campaign. The company expanded its product offerings to include home appliances and VCRs. Stores started to place all stock on the sales floor rather than in a stockroom, had fewer salespeople, and provided more self-help product information for its customers.

Best Buy also did away with salespeople working on commission, in order to make the shopping environment free of the high-pressure tactics used in other stores. In 2004, *Forbes* magazine named Best Buy as its "Company of the Year." The company grew rapidly. It introduced the innovative service team known as the Geek Squad[5] and eliminated mail-in rebates to address negative customer feedback. An increasing trend toward online shopping, however, began to erode revenues and profits in the 2010s.

Best Buy's biggest mistake seems to have been customer service failures. Customers routinely complained about bad experiences with pushy and unhelpful store employees. The customer service problem was compounded by Best Buy's lack of supply chain capabilities. It failed to ship thousands of preordered items that consumers planned to give as Christmas presents, and then failed to take responsibility for the failure.

The company's inventory management and reverse logistics systems for repair and return were notoriously bad. A lot of product sat unsold in stores. In the face of declining revenue, management aggressively cut costs and kept operations as lean as possible. This drove profit margins higher and kept investors happy in the short run. But a company can never achieve growth by cutting costs. To survive, Best Buy needed to have sustained sales growth, which could only be achieved by providing an improved customer experience. Unfortunately, Best Buy continued to focus on price promotion and expansion into consumer durables to attract customers but not so much on improving customer service.

INCREASING SERVICE LEVELS

Many companies improve customer service when they realize that product differentiation is not helping them sell more products, but they don't do it in a financially prudent way. When I ran sourcing projects for my clients, suppliers would provide free services as a way to sweeten the deal. Over time, it became an acceptable industry norm.

Take the example of the facility management[6] industry, which provides day-to-day employee services such as food preparation, janitorial, and office relocation. The suppliers charge their actual employee cost and add a management fee to account for their profit. The management fee is meant to ensure that suppliers are providing oversight for their operations. As competition became stiff, the suppliers started to put the fee at risk based on performance, and now it is an acceptable norm that the management fee will only be paid if the facility management supplier is doing everything right. This represented a drop from assured to completely at-risk profit. The risk profile of the facility management suppliers has increased, resulting in concern from their investors and customers about the sustainability of their offering.

Is a high service level necessarily bad? No. However, if your service levels do not vary by type of customer or if your customers are not willing to pay for better service, you are potentially overservicing your customers. Our experience across industries shows that companies seldom segment their service offerings, thereby allowing all of their customers access to the same high level of service. This results in significant cost increases when compared to the actual benefits from the increased level of service. Why does this happen? Costs are frequently not visible to customers, who are not offered incentives to choose the right service level. They end up asking for more service without considering the service cost.

The system works in a surprisingly similar way inside corporations as well. Many companies have set up their corporate functions, such as real estate, IT, HR, and procurement, as a shared services organization. The centralization effort is made with the hope that it will reduce costs through economies of scale. Instead, many firms are finding the costs of shared services going through the roof instead of coming down.

For example, a shared services organization at an aircraft company increased costs by 20% despite a decline in revenue. Why did this happen? It is hard to drive scale in the services area unless you completely restructure work processes. Also, the customer organizations better managed their expectations when they had to pay for their real estate or HR staff. They were okay with their offices being cleaned once every day. However, once centralized, the costs are shared by a larger pool, and no one challenges the need for an increased service level, such as getting the office cleaned immediately after a small spill. Without a disincentive, customers will continue to ask for better service even if they do not need it. It is similar to everyone ordering the most expensive dish on the menu at a dinner when the bill gets split equally.

To be known for service, a company should have intimate knowledge of customer needs, the ability to provide service that is difficult for its competition to match, and a way to get customers to pay for the better service.

TAILORING SERVICE LEVEL BY CUSTOMER SEGMENT

Most companies lack an understanding of the customer's need for service in different customer segments. Typically, only a small group of customers requires a high level of service. When faced with competition or customer requests, companies tend to increase the service level for all of their customer segments irrespective of their size or profitability.

For example, at one corporate bank, a group of customers was demanding a higher standard of service, which included having a personal banker, an investment specialist, 24/7 customer support, and other benefits.

The bank faced a distinct risk of losing these customers if it failed to provide an increased level of service because other banks were starting to market their services aggressively. To address the growing demand, the bank provided the improved service to all of its customers and did not charge for it. This resulted in a significant cost increase and impacted the bank's profitability.

Our analysis showed that only the segment of customers who maintained large investments with the bank was asking for the increased level of service. These customers were also willing to pay extra for the better service, which would have offset the increased cost. All the other customers were not that interested in the improved services, but they were willing to use them if they were provided at no extra cost. The bank would have managed its costs better if it had divided its customers into separate segments.

I have developed a three-step approach to separate customers by segment, define a menu of service levels, and match service levels with segments. It is a good way to think about service levels that can be offered to customers.

FIRST STEP—CLASSIFY CUSTOMERS BY SEGMENT

Most companies classify their customers for marketing or sales efforts. They use psychographic (lifestyle) or demographic segmentation to classify their customer base and identify the unique needs for developing products or services. However, these classifications are not useful to identify what service levels are needed to win in the market. Segmentation based on business metrics such as volume, profitability, or the strategic nature of an account has shown to be more useful. For example, Amazon Prime was targeted at customers who shop heavily online, irrespective of their lifestyle choices or demographics.

We were hired by a leading multibrand retailer to analyze its store delivery service costs. The costs were increasing rapidly, and the client wanted to know how it could fix the problem without compromising its operations. We found that its stores asked for increased delivery services from distributors without consideration to cost. The increased level of delivery service included daily servicing, using a dedicated truck, and delivering before 6 a.m. The service requests were made to optimize store labor but did not take into consideration the cost of delivery. It made sense to provide a higher level of service to premium locations and high-volume stores. But extending the same service to stores in remote locations created a significant cost burden. The distributor had to send partially filled trucks to service remote location stores, and it made no financial sense.

To analyze the problem, our team used a simple framework to segment stores for the retailer by defining their service levels (service-level agreements, or SLAs) in the Dallas market, which was chosen as a test market. The retailer had 85 stores, and all of them received the same level of service. We considered two important variables when determining the store segment. The first variable was store profitability and volume; the second variable was brand criticality (the degree to which the retailer wants to showcase certain stores). For brand criticality, think, for example, of the way Apple showcases its Fifth Avenue store in

Figure 1.1—Store Classification Matrix: SLA Requirements

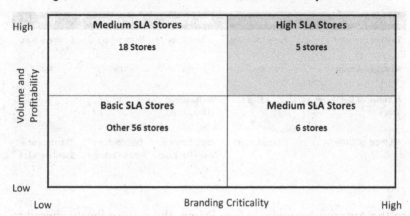

Manhattan. The segmentation showed that out of 85 stores only 5 stores needed a high level of service, 24 stores needed a medium level of service, and the rest could get by with a minimum threshold of service. High service levels typically involve delivery first thing in the morning and multiple deliveries in a week. Medium level of service may mean morning delivery and one to two deliveries in a week. A basic level of service may include delivery during the day and one delivery each week.

High service levels ensure that a store manager has all the required stock before the store opens and does not have to keep much inventory. Low service levels may inconvenience a store manager with receiving deliveries during the day and may mean holding a week's worth of inventory in the back room. Medium service levels are less inconvenient and require less inventory holding compared to low service levels. Our segmentation study showed that the retailer was overservicing 80 out of the 85 stores—or roughly 95% of stores in the Dallas area. See Figure 1.1.

SECOND STEP—DEVELOP A MENU OF SERVICE LEVELS

A menu of service levels is a list of different services that are either demanded by customers or provided by the competition. Going back

Figure 1.2—Multibrand Retailer Service Levels

Delivery Service	Current SLA	Aspirational	Competitors	Low
Time of Delivery	Early Morning	Morning	Before 5 p.m.	Before 5 p.m.
By Appointment	Yes	Yes	No	No
Number of Deliveries a Week	2 to 3	As Required, Unassisted	2 to 3	1
Method of Delivery	Distributor	Distributor + Small Package	Distributor + Small Package	Distributor + Small Package

to the Amazon example, before Prime, the service levels offered to customers were next-day, two-day, and seven-day delivery. Defining a menu of service levels involves doing a market survey to determine what is desired for particular products and services. In some cases, it may involve establishing a service level that is aspirational in nature.

At the multibrand retailer, we found that three different service levels were offered in the market, based on a wide variety of criteria. We also defined an aspirational service level, in which participating stores did not have to order; the required stock would be computed by the distributor and automatically supplied to them. See Figure 1.2.

THIRD STEP—IDENTIFY SERVICE LEVELS APPROPRIATE FOR DIFFERENT SEGMENTS

The third step is to identify service levels appropriate for different segments, which involves working with a target group of customers to identify the right service level for various segments. In some cases, it may require a simple discussion, and for others, it could include a focus group. In the case of the multi-brand retailer, we used a computer model to simulate the impact of different services on store performance. Our simulation effort showed that the current SLA was appropriate for high SLA stores, aspirational for medium SLA stores, and low for basic SLA stores. For basic SLA stores, the impact of the reduction of service was minimal on holding stock at stores or disruption to store operations.

DEVELOPING A COMPETITIVE EDGE

To be known for service, it is important to develop a model that is difficult for the competition to match. This is one of the sources of competitive advantage when product differentiation is low. Think about Southwest Airlines, whose product is very similar to other airlines', but what distinguishes the company is its service model.

Southwest Rapid Turnaround

The airline boasts timely arrivals and departures, 25-minute turnaround at the gate, and fewer technical problems. Airplanes make money in the air. Southwest has had 40+ years of profitability.[7] Its ability to get airplanes in and out of the gate faster than competitors explains part of the higher profitability. Southwest designed the whole process like a pit crew at the racetrack, where every second counts. The birth of the quick turnaround meant passengers and baggage were unloaded, the plane was cleaned and restocked, and the new passengers got on, all within the set time limit of 25 minutes. Everybody pitched in. Compare this to other airlines, which took an average 60 minutes to turn around their planes at the gate. Other airlines found it difficult to compete with the Southwest model because of their employment contracts.

In the case of the retailer, we realized that store managers were spending an enormous amount of time ordering products for their stores and coordinating delivery. The store team should be focused on managing the store and customers instead of spending time on coordination of deliveries. The aspirational model suggested by our team focused on removing the responsibility for delivery coordination from the store team. It meant negotiating with distributors and streamlining their supply chain. The distributor already had the store inventory and sales information, and it could use that information to plan deliveries and optimize routes. The delivery was scheduled to be made before stores opened and was to be kept in a secure holding area. The store manager could then choose to put the delivery items on the shelf first thing in the morning and focus on customers for the rest of the day. The distributor could change the frequency of delivery based on actual sales in the stores. Service capabilities were tested to ensure that the distributor was able to service the stores as planned.

GETTING CUSTOMERS TO PAY FOR INCREASED SERVICE

The key challenge is to determine how much the customer should be charged for service. This is hard to do, so companies use cost as a proxy. Even then, companies lack a complete understanding of the cost for different service levels. Most companies allocate service cost as a percentage of revenue and not based on the actual effort it took to deliver the service. For the same service level, the cost of service is the same irrespective of customer revenue. Charging customers a percentage of revenue results in higher-revenue customers being charged a higher price. This approach has two negative outcomes: It alienates higher-revenue customers and creates the wrong incentive for lower-revenue customers. In the case of the retailer store managers in remote locations they had no incentive to ask for reduced service, because they were not paying for the extra cost. Frankly, the store managers usually did not know the actual cost and were not able to make the right choices. Why did store managers not know the actual cost? Well, the invoices from distributors were complicated because they include shipments to a large number of disparate stores. The invoices provided cost based on trucks being dispatched but didn't break down the cost by store. A truck might end up servicing three to five stores in a day, and the route changed every day. Estimating the cost per store was complicated. So, the client didn't do it, and thus didn't know the cost for each store.

We created a cost model to help the client estimate costs based on the effort required to service different stores. It started with evaluating the components of the underlying cost structure. For example, for retail store delivery, the underlying cost includes labor, gas, and truck utilization. The cost varied by miles driven, similar to the way it works with cars. The cost for a car depends to a large extent on how many miles the car is driven. The IRS gives a deduction based on the number of miles the car has been driven for business. However, our retailer had negotiated with its distributors a rate based on a shipment's weight. The distributor was incentivized to carry more loads and had no incentive to make the routes more efficient. We had to renegotiate the pricing structure with the distributor to align it with the new service model.

The cost model provided insight into the delivery cost structure for different service levels. It showed that the retailer spent $44,000 to service each of its 85 stores every week. Competitors were paying on average $24,000, or nearly half. The cost differential was a genuine concern for the retailer. The analysis also showed that dropping the service level to an aspirational level would reduce the cost to $27,000. It would bring the service cost in line with what competitors were paying for store delivery but would also result in relatively better service for the retailer's stores. Lowering the service level further would lead to a delivery cost of only $16,000. That was close to half of what competitors were paying for their service delivery. Figure 1.3 provides an illustration of cost for different service levels.

The exercise of reclassifying stores and mapping the right service levels reduced the average store delivery cost to $20,600 from $44,000, a 55% reduction without impacting store operations. It was below the cost competitors were paying to service their stores.

The exercise provided the actual cost of delivery to the retailer. Instead of imposing service levels on their stores, the management asked store managers to choose the service levels appropriate for their stores

Figure 1.3—Service Levels and Associated Costs

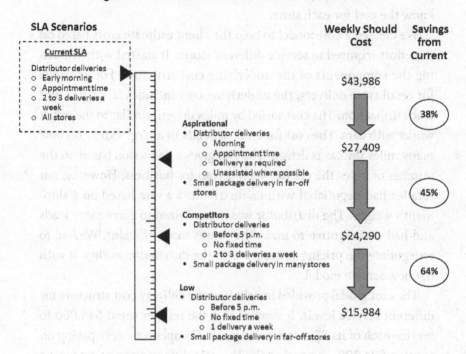

SLA Scenarios

Current SLA

Distributor deliveries
o Early morning
o Appointment time
o 2 to 3 deliveries a week
o All stores

Weekly Should Cost

$43,986

Savings from Current

38%

Aspirational
• Distributor deliveries
  o Morning
  o Appointment time
  o Delivery as required
  o Unassisted where possible
• Small package delivery in far-off stores

$27,409

45%

Competitors
• Distributor deliveries
  o Before 5 p.m.
  o No fixed time
  o 2 to 3 deliveries a week
• Small package delivery in many stores

$24,290

64%

Low
• Distributor deliveries
  o Before 5 p.m.
  o No fixed time
  o 1 delivery a week
• Small package delivery in far-off stores

$15,984

and also to pay for the cost associated with delivery. Store managers were responsible for individual store profitability. As store managers reviewed the cost of delivery, most chose the service levels that were predicted by the store classification study. There were two exceptions. Store managers felt the need to increase service levels when they were running promotions. Also, they were willing to pay for higher costs during the Christmas holidays. Since they knew when these events were planned in any calendar year, they were able to provide advanced notice to the distributor. The distributor's incentives then aligned with store delivery requirements, and they were able to hire additional staff during the peak season. The overall costs were reduced by half, with significant improvement in service to the stores.

IMPROVING SERVICE WITH THE HELP OF SUPPLY CHAIN

Below are key questions that every company, from a small-scale business to a global corporation, needs to ask about its customer service:

- **How do you measure customer service?** Companies measure customer service through surveys that measure satisfaction with the service provided to customers. Improving customer service has been shown to retain and increase customer base. It is a powerful tool if you are in a highly competitive market or when customers are fickle. A better way to measure customer service is by focusing on loyalty of the customer base, that is, money spent by existing customers or renewal of membership.

- **Are you focusing on customer-facing employees or underlying operations to improve customer service?** Most companies assume that modifying scripts or providing more training or adding more staff to customer-facing organizations will enhance customer service. They are sadly mistaken. It requires improving underlying operations to meet or exceed customer requirements and doing this in a cost-effective fashion.

- **Are you able to improve service in a cost-effective manner?** When challenged to improve customer service, most companies do it with increasing costs, which impacts profitability. They soon find it hard to sustain the higher levels of service. They tend to offer one service standard to all customers, thereby underservicing critical segments and overservicing less critical segments. This approach results in increased cost and loss of satisfaction among customers who are essential for growth and profitability. Also, most companies fail to get customers to pay for the increased service despite the customers' willingness to do so.

■ **Is your service model unique and difficult for competitors to copy?** To win in customer service, companies have to develop a unique service model that competitors find difficult to copy. Otherwise, the advantage will be short lived and become industry standard, thereby increasing the cost for everyone. Developing a unique service model requires a deep understanding of customer requirements and the in-house operations that would be required.

■ **What's the best way to improve customer service?** To improve customer service, companies should segment customers, define and map service levels by segments, create a service model that is hard for the competition to match, and then convince customers to pay for the increased service. Supply chain organizations are involved in the delivery and can help in defining unique service models and estimating cost.

■ **Do you include supply chain organization in customer service discussions?** Improving customer service is a team sport that requires participation and coordination among different functional groups. Unfortunately, supply chain organizations are typically kept out of service-level discussions. Most CEOs consider the supply chain as a support organization that is responsible for delivering services that the sales team promised to customers. Not involving the supply chain has created a significant problem for some companies. For example, at a high-tech company, the sales team promised to deliver hardware to a customer with remote locations in Europe within two days of being ordered. The customer included a severe penalty clause in the contract to ensure that the services were performed as promised. The high-tech company's supply chain organization was not geared up to service all the locations across Europe. Its distributors were not able to deliver the hardware within the required two days to all of the remote locations. This created a lot of complaints from different locations as the sales representatives showed up without hardware. The high-tech company had to fly service representatives to remote locations. It was a mess. The company ended up paying a lot of money to the customer as a penalty.

It undoubtedly helps for supply chain organizations not just to be involved but to lead the service discussion. Though the sales and marketing team can help in classifying customers, the supply chain organization can point to different service models that can be offered to the client. They can also estimate the cost and effort associated with delivering the service. The sales team then can negotiate the price with the customer.

In addition to improving customer service, companies can boost revenue by bringing innovation quickly to market and being responsive to market demand. In the next chapter, we will review how supply chain can improve delivery of innovation by making customization, global sourcing, and market-driven planning a reality.

2

BOOST REVENUE WITH SUPPLY CHAIN

THE AIRBUS SUPPLY CHAIN ADVANTAGE

Boeing, one of the most innovative aviation companies, had a problem bringing its innovation to market. Ultimately, its inability to streamline its supply chain caused it to lose its innovation edge over European rival Airbus. The challenges faced by Boeing are not unique to the aircraft industry. In fact, companies struggle with similar issues in many other industries that rely on innovation, be it high tech, consumer goods, pharmaceuticals, or medical devices.

The challenges stem from three factors: (1) customization or personalization, which increases complexity; (2) globalization, which increases lead time; and (3) demand planning that relies on forecasts instead of actual customer demand. A supply chain specifically tailored to a company's business model addresses these challenges effectively and, in turn, boosts revenue and profits. The company that embraces supply chain efficiency will enjoy a market advantage.

Let's look at why Airbus enjoys supply chain advantage over Boeing.

THE RISE OF BOEING

William Edward Boeing was an American aviation pioneer who founded a global giant in the construction of advanced aircraft. The company shined under the leadership of Clairmont Egtvedt, Boeing's chief engineer. He famously told his boss that "we are building airplanes, not cement sidewalks," meaning that the company might as well be in the concrete business unless it was willing to let its engineering staff have a free hand in designing new aircraft.

Boeing had the wisdom to accept Egtvedt's challenge, and Egtvedt had the brains and foresight to produce pioneering aircraft designs, including the Stratoliner, the Flying Fortress, and the Superfortress.

After Egtvedt became company president in 1933, engineering and design became Boeing's hallmark. Egtvedt envisioned a future of large passenger planes and cutting-edge military aircraft. Under Egtvedt's guidance, Boeing not only introduced revolutionary designs, but also developed a supply chain that would help Boeing turn out aircraft in large numbers by forming collaborations with other companies.

During World War II, production jumped from 60 planes per month in 1942 to an extraordinary 360 planes per month by March 1944. The company even turned out 16 planes in one 24-hour period, part of the Herculean American supply effort that was credited with helping to win the war. Today Boeing is a giant with $100 billion in revenue and $5 billion in after-tax profit, having acquired most of its U.S. rivals in the commercial space. It has produced the 737, 747, 787, and other groundbreaking aircraft designs. The company epitomizes innovation.

Although Boeing has retained its focus on the need to be innovative in aircraft design, it lost focus on the need to innovate its supply chain. In fact, the updating and improvement of supply chain capabilities were ignored. This was a mistake and turned out to be Boeing's Achilles' heel.

INNOVATION AND SUPPLY CHAIN

Companies spend billions of dollars every year on innovation. Many mistakenly believe that innovation is only about designing cool products and services. They hire the best engineers, designers, artists, and architects but fail to invest in organizations and processes that are critical in making the design a reality. One of the organizations that is not given importance is supply chain. For innovation to reach the market, the parts have to be procured from suppliers, the product has to be assembled or manufactured in plants, and then it has to be delivered to customers in a cost-effective way. The challenges do not end here. If the products are successful, the supply chain should be able to scale quickly to meet increasing demand, service them during use, and remove them postuse.

Supply chain can make innovations successful and provide an advantage when the company may not be first to the market. It is like having a great engine and transmission in a good-looking sports car. The things that are not visible on the surface are what make you win the race.

AIRBUS ENTERS THE MARKET

The European consortium Airbus, formed in 1970, became Boeing's main competitor in commercial aviation and soon achieved a cost advantage over Boeing because of its more advanced supply chain and superior sourcing expertise. Some people assumed that Airbus must be winning in the market because of government subsidies. Not so. Several studies showed that the advantage of Airbus stemmed from its superior supply chain.

For Boeing, the major challenge was to simplify aircraft design and to move from ground-up production to subassemblies and modular design.

Airbus's aircraft designs are simple and easy to manufacture. Instead of building a plane from the ground up at one location, Airbus produces subassemblies at factories in Britain, Spain, France, and Germany, and then assembles them into finished aircraft in France. This so-called assembly production approach depends on modular design, versus Boeing's ground-up approach, which requires custom construction of each airplane as if it were a specialized race car. It is sometimes assumed that Airbus has an advantage because it produces everything in-house. Boeing also produced most of its major components in-house. Airbus, by contrast, moved to modular design. By using this design approach, Airbus enjoyed a competitive advantage over Boeing.

The benefits of using modular design are well documented: Modular design is easy to manage, keeps inventories low, improves manufacturing quality, and lowers overall costs. The success of this approach, however, depends on two prerequisites: The overall design has to be set by the original equipment manufacturer (OEM) early on, and the subassembly manufacturers need the flexibility to make design changes on their own initiative, as long as these do not detract from overall performance.

With a modular assembly, the component design challenges move from the OEM to the subassembly manufacturer. Boeing, however, did not know how to properly implement a modular design, whether the subassemblies were made in-house or by suppliers. Boeing engineers designed and managed production down to the component level, which diminished the flexibility and accountability of the subassembly manufacturers. Boeing's engineers also had a habit of getting into supplier processes. Prototype testing became more elaborate and critical to ensure that all parts fit well together. The process consequently could not be rushed. Airbus claims to have created a digital mock-up of A350 XB, which serves as the master reference for the entire team working on this next-generation jetliner.[8] The digital mock-up speeds up the aircraft's development, providing access to all participants (internal and external), who work as a virtual team no matter where they are located. It reduces the probability of error and parts not fitting each other at a later time.

Going forward, unless Boeing masters the modular design approach, the company will probably remain at a competitive disadvantage with Airbus and will continue to lose market share. Boeing's long-term survival depends on revamping its supply chain. The Department of Defense is now asking all participants for the design of the U.S. Air Force's Long-Range Striker Bomber to develop in modules. This will allow future incremental modifications on the aircraft's systems. The modular design concept is likely to be rolled out to all future aircraft design whether military or civilian.

BOEING PLAYS CATCH-UP

An example of Boeing's nearsightedness with regard to supply chain was the way it tried to build the 787 Dreamliner.

The 787 is a long-range aircraft that was meant to allow direct flights between cities and render the current airline "hub-and-spoke" model obsolete. It was designed to be 20% more fuel efficient than the 767, which it was intended to replace. To achieve this savings, the aircraft's airframe was designed to be built primarily with lightweight composite materials.

The plane also had many other innovations, such as electrical flight systems, swept wings, and noise-reducing chevrons on its engines. Boeing planned to assemble the 787 from large subassemblies, rather than building it from the ground up in the traditional manner. This was the first time Boeing used subassemblies in a large aircraft design.

Subassemblies for the Dreamliner were constructed by some of the best suppliers globally, with wings manufactured in Japan, passenger doors built in France, cargo doors in Sweden, wiring from France, and

Figure 2.1—Global Partners for 787

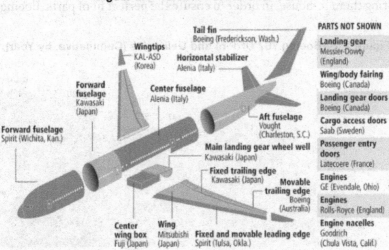

Source: Boeing 787 Dreamliner assembly

software developed in India. See Figure 2.1. This was Boeing's effort to play catch-up with Airbus's superior supply chain.

But Boeing's engineering culture was not a good fit with the subassembly approach. It was like mixing oil and water. Boeing struggled to make the deadlines for the 787 launch. Initial deliveries to All Nippon Airways (ANA), a Japanese airline, were planned to start in 2008, but the first deliveries were not made until September 2011. Even after the launch, Boeing was not able to produce the 787 in sufficient quantities to complete its order book. Figure 2.2 shows orders for the 787 versus actual deliveries.

The first 787s were delivered to ANA on September 25, 2011, three years behind schedule.

What went wrong? Almost every major technological advance, of course, has teething issues. But the Dreamliner's problems were exacerbated by Boeing's implementation of its decision to buy parts from outside contractors. Some parts did not fit together properly. Shims used to bridge small parts were not attached correctly. Some aircraft had to have their tails extensively reworked.

Unions blamed the delays on the company's reliance on outsourcing. Boeing eventually was forced to buy some of its suppliers and to bring them in-house, in order to ensure the perfect fit of parts. Boeing

Figure 2.2—Boeing 787 Orders and Deliveries (Cumulative, by Year)

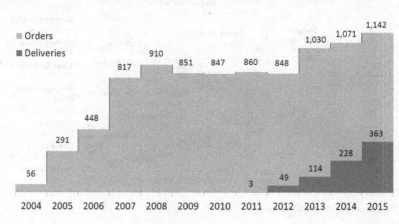

Source: Boeing

President and Chief Executive Jim McNerney defended the decision to outsource. In an analyst conference, he mentioned, "It's not just our supplier's fault. It is equally our fault. In some cases, we asked partners to do some things they were not technically or financially able to do when you look back with 20/20 hindsight. I would draw the lines in a different place, use more shared engineering, and have more visibility on the supply chain across corporate boundaries."

A *Harvard Business Review* article agreed with McNerney's view and said the problem was not so much the outsourcing as it was the decision to modularize a complicated problem too soon. The author said, "[T]he issues the plane (787) has been facing have much more to do with Boeing's decision to treat the design and production of such a radically new and different aircraft as a modular system so early in its development."[9]

Why did Boeing struggle with a supply chain concept that appears to work well at Airbus? There are three issues.

Customization Philosophy

Because of Boeing's history with military aviation, its engineers focus on performance, with little consideration for the difficulty of manufacturing or procuring parts. The situation is similar to the problems designers of race cars face when trying to build a commercial car: Each and every part is custom made with very tight tolerance.

Airbus, on the other hand, takes a very practical approach toward design. Its engineers tend to design components that are easy to manufacture and supply. Also, they use many of the same components in different airplane models.

There is a striking difference of approach between Boeing and Airbus suppliers. Boeing suppliers tend to have precision and stand-alone machine tools that have high overhead costs. The company is dependent primarily on a single source for producing a particular component and has no backup if something goes wrong with a key supplier. Airbus suppliers, on the other hand, tend to have all-purpose mass-manufacturing machine tools. This makes it easy for Airbus to distribute its work among suppliers and reroute projects if something goes wrong with one manufacturer.

Long Lead Time

Boeing distributed its supply chain across the globe in order to find the best and brightest suppliers. But this created problems with language and culture and was extremely hard to coordinate. Also, Boeing engineers were notorious for making multiple design changes, with some coming at the very last minute with little to no input from the suppliers. Many of these design changes achieved only incremental benefits but created havoc with the suppliers' plans.

Unless a supplier had worked with Boeing before, it became difficult for suppliers to manage this constant change philosophy. In addition, choosing a new set of suppliers with different cultures and communication challenges was a recipe for disaster for Boeing. System integration and testing became an issue: Implementing change takes time when you are working with suppliers in different parts of the world. In a rush to meet the deadline for launch, corners were sometimes cut, which resulted in post launch problems.

Demand Planning and Communication

Many of Boeing's problems could be traced back to its failure to communicate its requirements and demand data to suppliers. Nuts and bolts suppliers were often unaware of increased demand and, accordingly, failed to change their output capacity.

In December 2014, Airbus shipped its first A350 XWB aircraft, a long-range wide-body jet, to Qatar Airways, in direct competition with Boeing's 787. Boeing initially had a 10- to 11-year advantage over Airbus, which could have given Boeing significant installed product base before Airbus was able to launch a competitive product. But due to

Boeing's supply chain problems, Airbus rapidly caught up. This was a big problem for a company that invested billions of dollars in R&D and expected to pay for it by premium pricing in the initial years. Boeing may never fully recoup its investment.

The Securities and Exchange Commission is now investigating Boeing for the way in which it accounted for the program costs of the 787 and 747 jetliners.[10] Boeing seemed to have spread its R&D costs over several years to make its financials look good. If Boeing is unable to get 787 and 747 sales, spreading these investments over several years gives a false sense of profitability to investors. This is a concern for the Securities and Exchange Commission, and Boeing's share price dropped by 7% in one day in February 2016. Boeing is said to be cutting costs by trimming its labor force to compensate for the perceived drop in profitability.

Tell that to anyone who says supply chain issues aren't worth the cost to fix.

The supply chain can help companies achieve their revenue target by continuing to respond to market demand quickly while enabling business choices. Business models may vary from one company to another in the same industry; supply chains have to be tailored to each company, so they deliver the results expected from them. Companies need to find a balance between competing priorities. They can accomplish this by:

- Separating the supply chain by demand patterns to manage customization
- Simplifying their network, storing inventory strategically, and having flexible terms with suppliers to enable global sourcing
- Allowing market demand to pull the products from factories, thereby matching production capacity with market demand

Let me elaborate these points in more detail.

MAKING CUSTOMIZATION A REALITY

With the advent of online retailing, the concept of mass customization is gaining ground. This, in a nutshell, means companies can now tailor their products and services for the individual customer, en masse.

Although mass customization has yet to be fully implemented, companies have tried hard to provide a greater breadth of goods and services to consumers with the hope of winning them over. This process has resulted in a proliferation of new products. Take, for example, the iPhone. Apple launched the iPhone as one product, but a few years after the first launch, we have many variations in terms of generation, color, size, and memory.

The supply chain has to meet the demand of each of these product variations so that each consumer order is fulfilled at the right time and place. This is no easy task because each product is unique in some ways. The phones have different components, such as the CPU, camera, and screen, depending on the product's generation, memory size, and case color. The whole process has become highly complex. If the iPhone example is not complex enough for you, imagine a cosmetic product such as lipstick, with hundreds of color variations, sizes, and packaging differences. Imagine the complexity of managing the supply process to ensure the right product is available at the right place.

There is another aspect of customization that gets introduced by design engineers. Take, for example, Boeing's design philosophy. The larger the number of parts to be produced or purchased from suppliers, the more complex the supply chain. Someone has to order, maintain, and produce the parts to ensure that the final products are shipped to customers on time.

Most companies have tried to create platforms that share common parts so that only a minimum number of parts needs to be customized for the finished product.

Also, the process often depends on where the customization is happening. At computer companies, customization typically happens at the manufacturing site. Motherboards and computer cases may be different, but most component parts that go into a computer are similar. They are configured differently for gaming, office, and home computers. So supply chain planners have to worry about a demand versus capacity mismatch at their own assembly plants, but not so much on the suppliers' end.

In aircraft manufacturing, however, customization happens at the supplier level. This means that the suppliers have to buy specialized equipment to manufacture the parts. Capacity planning and investment guarantees become an issue. Someone has to worry about demand and capacity mismatch not only at the aircraft companies' plants but also at the supplier end. In the case of military equipment, customization even happens at Tier 2 suppliers, meaning the suppliers' suppliers. This brings in an added level of complexity because the possibility of a demand/capacity mismatch goes much deeper in the supply chain, and there is a greater need for coordination among everyone involved.

Does customization help increase sales? The answer is yes. The days of the Model T Ford, when they made one product for everyone, are long gone. Do many product variations help? There is always a debate about the right number of product variations. However, one thing is certain: Without offering sufficient customization, companies will find it difficult to compete in today's marketplace.

How can a supply chain help? The supply chain can improve a company's ability to customize by doing two things: influencing upstream R&D process and segmenting supply chain by demand pattern.

INFLUENCE UPSTREAM R&D PROCESS

First, the supply chain works with R&D and the sales team while products are being designed to ensure the assumptions made at the design stage are practical. Companies use big data to tease out consumer insights and drive their product design strategies. Supply chain folks are typically not involved at that point, when many assumptions are being made about costs and capabilities needed to launch. The supply chain can beneficially influence product design strategies by helping estimate costs and providing feedback on different assumptions. Figure 2.3 is an example of the aircraft manufacturing industry where a large portion of the cost is in overhead and non–value added.

Why does overhead represent so much of the cost? Because suppliers, in order to customize at their level, have to invest in specialized machines and tooling. This equipment has lower utilization rates because order quantities are typically small. There is a significant wait time between orders. In some cases, suppliers retool the equipment to produce a different product—and retooling takes time.

To avoid the downtime for retooling, aircraft companies try to hold inventory across the supply chain. This in turn impacts supply chain responsiveness to market demand when demand is lower than capacity. In high-demand years, a huge backlog can develop and the time required for adding capacity can be great due to the specialized nature of the equipment. It is very common for both Boeing and Airbus to have several years of order backlogs.

To avoid this problem, Airbus introduced a subassembly concept that allowed suppliers to reduce overhead costs by better managing

Figure 2.3—Aerospace Industry: Cost Structure

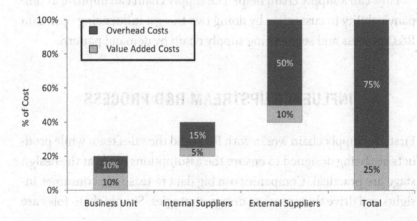

the design. This concept could run into problems if suppliers failed to coordinate their design choices with each other. This is particularly true for Boeing, where design changes are frequent and made with little to no input from suppliers. You can see why the 787 had problems with parts from different suppliers not fitting together properly.

Is this problem unique to the aircraft industry? No. I hear similar complaints from other industries with a long lead time for research and development, such as automobiles, pharma, or consumer goods.

SEGMENT SUPPLY CHAIN BY DEMAND PATTERN

It is important that supply chain organizations have an effective way of managing customization. Most companies have single do-it-all supply chains, which, like most do-it-all concepts, do not do anything very well and can get bogged down. Now imagine supply chains that cater to disparate demand patterns differently. This means having separate supply chains based on fast-moving, slow-moving, and customized products. It is about breaking the supply chain in multiple parallel flows so that each flow can be optimized for the type of demand. Think of car manufacturing. GM, Ford, and others have factories for their fast-moving products, which use robots that are laid out along an assembly line. It is highly cost-efficient and throughput focused. For slow-moving items (such as snap-in upgrades), it makes sense to have a modular design. So, depending on what's ordered, the manufacturer can switch the modules to create the finished product. This approach avoids holding up the manufacturing line if a module is not in inventory and completes the order when modules become available. See Figure 2.4.

At home, we have toasters, stoves, and microwaves to cater to different breakfast requirements in the morning. If we had only one appliance to make breakfast, how complex would it have to be to meet everyone's breakfast needs? How long would it take to make everyone's breakfast?

Figure 2.4—
Benefits of Separated vs. "One-Size-Fits-All" Supply Chain

"One-Size-Fits-All" Supply Chain

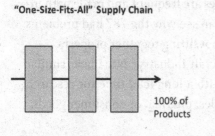

100% of
Products

A single flow for all businesses leads to optimize
for worst-case scenario
- Complex flows to accommodate the unknown
- Complex systems to reprioritize and expedite
  o Extra just-in-case capacity

Total Cost = X

Separated Supply Chain

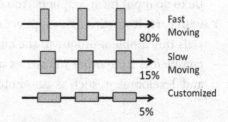

Fast
Moving
80%

Slow
Moving
15%

Customized
5%

Separated supply chain match requirements of
different customer and product segments, e.g.:
- Fast moving—assembly line approach
- Slow moving—cellular manufacturing
  approach/modular design
- Customized—ground up production

Total Cost = X/3

Similarly, studies have shown that separating the supply chain by demand pattern can significantly increase throughput, improve quality, and reduce costs. The decision on where to separate the supply chain depends on where customization is happening in the supply chain. For most high-tech companies, it probably makes sense to have a supply chain separate from manufacturing sites because components that go into making computers are similar. On the other hand, aircraft manufacturers and defense contractors probably need to think about separating their supply chain at their supplier or supplier's supplier, depending on where the customization is happening. It requires significant planning and discipline. If done well, it can reduce cost, improve responsiveness, and provide an important competitive edge to companies.

ENABLING GLOBAL SOURCING

Companies have taken advantage of globalization by sourcing cheaper products and labor from the developing world. Many have moved their manufacturing to China and other parts of the Asia-Pacific region. These moves have no doubt helped companies tap into lower-cost resources. However, they have also stretched the supply chain, which, in turn, has increased cycle time.[11]

Trade across borders is not easy. Customs and other requirements, though simplified by trade agreements, still pose a hurdle. Managing multiple modes of transportation (sea, land, and air) also presents its share of challenges. The longer the supply chain, the bigger the impact of any change. We call this the "whiplash" effect. The cascading impact of a small outage or failure at one end of the supply chain can have a significant impact on the other end.

You may have read about the massive impact the March 2011 Fukushima earthquake and tsunami had on the Japanese electronics industry and the desperate efforts by Apple executives to ensure sufficient supplies to maintain inventories. Japanese companies such as Sony, Toshiba, and others ran out of stock, and it took them months to develop backup suppliers and get production back online. Apple enjoyed a significant advantage in the market during that period.

Some companies do end-of-month or end-of-quarter sales promotions. It becomes tough to estimate demand for these events, which typically create a ripple effect through the supply chain. The longer the supply chain, the more problems promotion strategies create for factories and suppliers.

Is longer cycle time necessarily bad for business? Not really, but the supply chain should be able to manage the longer cycle effectively. Otherwise, the extra time can create severe problems. A shorter cycle time, of course, helps the supply chain to respond to market changes better.

How can a company reduce cycle time? It is prudent to review the supply chain network periodically. Over time, the flow of goods becomes more complicated as companies add new products, warehouses, and third-party suppliers. Reviewing the network ensures it is optimized for the current situation. Sometimes it is better to keep a few months of inventory of long lead time items, to protect against any supply problems.

Building a computer model of the supply chain has shown to be the best way to respond to demand changes. The model can be used to analyze the flow of all materials through the complex supply chain and then to optimize the flow. With today's computer technology, these modeling efforts are relatively straightforward.

Figure 2.5 is an illustration of network simplification at a consumer goods company in India. Which one do you think is easier to manage: the one before the network review, shown at left, or after? The simplification reduced the time from manufacturing to market from four months to two months. It reduced finished good inventory by half and improved freshness of the product.

It makes sense also to reduce the time necessary to change from producing one product to another at the factory as well as the minimum production size. This measure will reduce inventory and wait time for the product. While this sounds obvious, many companies do not review their network periodically. Pharmaceutical companies sometimes head in the opposite direction. They increase the length of the production run by increasing batch sizes[12] in their factories. This

Figure 2.5—Network Simplifications: Streamlining of Material Flow

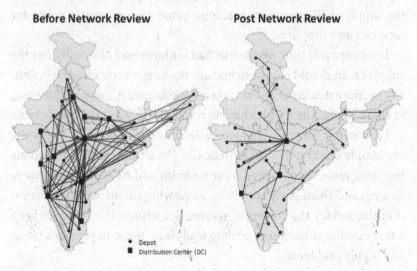

Before Network Review   Post Network Review

● Depot
■ Distribution Center (DC)

reduces the cost of production but, unfortunately, increases inventory and reduces the flexibility to change from one product to another quickly.

Additionally, when suppliers agree to provide quicker responses and transaction processing is simplified, cycle time is reduced. While companies have outsourced a substantial portion of their supply chains to external providers, such as contract manufacturers or third-party logistics providers, they often fail to add incentives to contracts with suppliers that allow them to respond quickly to demand changes.

Transaction processing in many companies is a mess. The process for ordering goods is frequently very complicated, with multiple levels of required approvals and complex links to budget processes. These procedures are designed to reduce risk by eliminating errors. But they inadvertently increase the time required to respond to changes in the market and overhead costs for everyone. At a high-tech company, we found that the order-processing time was twice that required by suppliers to actually deliver the product. The orders routinely got held up in bureaucratic procedures and waiting for multiple approvals at the company. The approval process significantly slowed the ability of the organization to respond to market changes and required frequent expediting of orders internally and with suppliers to meet deadlines.

MOVING TO DEMAND-DRIVEN PLANNING

Demand-driven planning refers to the short-term process for replenishment of goods, and not medium- or long-term planning for capacity. Most companies forecast market demand based on historical information to ship or replenish goods to distributors and retailers. Yet forecasts based on history miss the mark half of the time, giving you approximately the same odds of being right as if you'd flipped a coin. Forecasts based on historical data are never going to be accurate, because history is not a good predictor of future events. Things change—competitive action, consumer taste or preference, and changes in disposable income have an impact on consumer demand, so it is difficult to forecast. Even with supercomputers, weather forecasting beyond a week is still highly inaccurate.

Forecasting based on historical data is like driving your car while looking in the rearview mirror. As with driving a car, it is better to look at the road ahead to plan for shipments. Real-time demand information provides better insight into customer demand and can be used for shipment planning. This is true when customer demand data is readily available. Companies can ask their customers to provide future demand/orders. If that is not possible, then firms can estimate the demand based on a customer's production plans and inventory levels. For selling to consumers, companies can use actual order information as a trigger for shipment and production instead of using forecasts. As demand information becomes more reliable, inventory can be reduced, and capacity can be freed up for new product launches. The motto should be "Don't produce if the product is not selling." Otherwise, the product will occupy warehouse space, and then be either written off or sold at a discount, diluting the brand value.

How does this process work? Think about a series of bins. When someone picks an item from the first bin, then the bin behind sends an item to replenish the first bin. This process cascades through the whole series of bins. So, what happens, in reality, is customer demand pulls the products through the supply chain. It creates pull through warehouses, factories, and at the supplier end. It is very different from the traditional approach, where products are pushed to customers by factories producing goods based on a forecast. See Figure 2.6 for a small illustration of how it works.

Let's look at a real-life example of the benefits of pull-based replenishment. A leading consumer goods company implemented pull-based replenishment, which allowed it to triple the number of its new product introductions and to significantly increase sales organization productivity.

Inventory dropped by half as demand became more predictable. Also, capacity increased by 30% because of the reduced production

Figure 2.6—Push vs. Pull System for Shipment

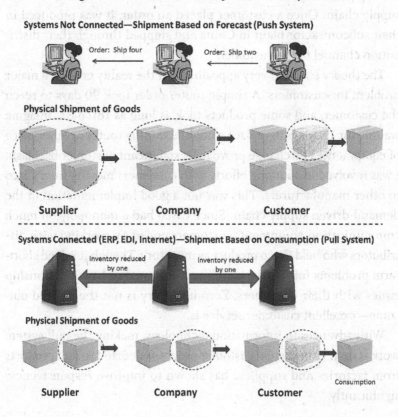

Systems Not Connected—Shipment Based on Forecast (Push System)

Order: Ship four   Order: Ship two

Physical Shipment of Goods

Supplier   Company   Customer

Systems Connected (ERP, EDI, Internet)—Shipment Based on Consumption (Pull System)

Inventory reduced by one   Inventory reduced by one

Physical Shipment of Goods

Supplier   Company   Customer   Consumption

of nonmoving products. The decline in inventory and increased capacity allowed the company to introduce new products every month versus once every quarter. Pull-based replenishment removed order management work from the sales team, and they started focusing on selling to customers.

Many people confuse pull-based planning with a "zero inventory" process. They become concerned about not having enough stock if something goes wrong with their supply chain. The objective of pull-based planning is to provide excellent customer service while reducing inventory (not having zero inventory). The role of the supply chain is to provide a balance between competing objectives.

Cisco is an excellent case study of this process. After scrapping nonmoving inventory in 2001, Cisco decided to move to a made-to-order supply chain. Once a customer placed an order, it was produced in their subcontractor plant in China and shipped through their distribution channel to the customer.

The theory sounded very appealing, but the reality created a major problem for customers. A simple router order took 90 days to reach the customer, and some products took as long as 180 days. Imagine waiting for 180 days to replace a nonfunctioning router or other piece of equipment! The change provoked a significant customer backlash. I was involved in sourcing efforts with customers moving from Cisco to other manufacturers. This was not a good implementation of the demand-driven supply chain. Since Cisco had a monopoly on much communication equipment, customers ended up working with distributors who held Cisco product as inventory. Though it solved short-term problems for customers, Cisco continued to have relationship issues with their customers. Zero inventory is not the desired outcome—excellent customer service is.

With advances in information technology, making the pull system work is easy. Using actual customer orders or demand to pull products from factories and suppliers has shown to improve responsiveness significantly.

BOOSTING REVENUE WITH SUPPLY CHAIN

Innovation involves both design and delivery. Many companies focus their efforts on design and don't invest in their capability to deliver, which ends up becoming their Achilles' heel. They fail to strengthen their ability to manufacture, maintain, and return. Also, they fail to create a competitive cost structure. These deficiencies reduce revenue and profit potential once competitors catch up with their products in the market. A supply chain tailored to a company's business model can make innovation successful and provide an enduring competitive edge.

- The supply chain can boost revenue by enabling customization or personalization, sourcing from global suppliers, and responsiveness to market demand.
- Customization increases revenue, but it also increases complexity and cost. Separating supply chain by demand pattern can help companies manage increasing complexity and cost.
- Globalization allowed businesses to benefit from supplier innovation and lower cost, but it increased lead time and logistical challenges. Supply chain can make global sourcing work by simplifying network, storing inventory strategically, and having flexible terms with suppliers.
- Supply chain can improve responsiveness to customer demand by replenishing based on customer demand and reducing reliance on the forecast. This can be achieved by pulling products from factories and suppliers based on demand, and also by shortening lead time.
- To boost revenue, the supply chain organization will have to step up its game. It is important to understand that the implementation process can take years. Clearly, there needs to be a mandate from both corporate and supply chain leadership. It can be difficult to get buy-in to fix things that are not manifestly broken. Leadership commitment and tenacity are keys to moving the supply chain to a better state. The message needs to emphasize that the changes are not merely a Band-Aid and, like any permanent fix, they will deliver results for years to come.

For the supply chain organization, implementation will require a new skill set. Currently, supply chain organization members are often more focused on planning—whether it is demand planning, sales and operation planning, production planning, or supply planning. Moving to a responsive supply chain will require significant modeling skills to optimize the network and reduce cycle time and variability. Collaboration and teamwork skills will be needed to work effectively with R&D and sales and marketing teams in the upstream innovation process. These organizations thrive on creative thinking, and successful collaboration will require the ability to think laterally instead of simply following current practices.

Successful collaboration will also require an excellent understanding of both fixed and variable costs and their drivers. Acquiring the skills and knowledge that will be needed will take time, and companies will have to invest in training to achieve the desired results.

In addition to boosting revenue, there is another way for companies to increase revenue, and that is by joining hands with other companies. Gone are the days when companies could do everything in-house. With ecosystem changes and as technology disrupts industries, alliances and partnerships can provide a powerful competitive advantage. In the next chapter, we will discuss how sourcing organizations can make alliances successful.

3

AMPLIFY ALLIANCE PERFORMANCE WITH SOURCING

ALLIANCES CAN MAKE OR BREAK A COMPANY

Business alliances have fallen out of favor these days. Leading companies, such as Google, Tesla, Microsoft, and Pfizer, are trying to do everything in-house. If the capabilities don't exist in-house, they acquire other companies. This is done with the belief that management will have better control of in-house resources and avoid the distraction of managing an external organization that doesn't understand the company's culture. Does this strategy work? Well, the strategy works in the company's field of core expertise, but fails as it tries to diversify. Look at the number of acquisitions that have been written off by many of the leading companies.

Unlike acquisitions, alliances take advantage of differences. If designed correctly, alliances can help all of the parties involved to achieve common goals, which they may fail to reach on their own. Alliances are like marriages. They require not only proper courtship but also ongoing relationship management. The ability to negotiate a win-win deal and having an effective alliance management process can make alliances successful. Most leaders take their eyes off the ball once a deal is signed and fail to put together an effective management process, which results in alliance failure. CEOs rarely involve sourcing organizations in making alliances work. But sourcing can help with deal negotiations and the ongoing partnership management.

ART OF ALLIANCE—STARBUCKS STYLE

One of the biggest proponents of alliances has been Howard Schultz. He bought Starbucks coffee from its original owners in 1987. Sales of mass-produced coffee beans by Folgers and other brands were declining, whereas specialty coffee was becoming popular. "When I first discovered the Italian espresso bars on my trip to Italy, the vision was to re-create that for America—a third place that had not existed before," Schultz later recalled. "Starbucks re-created that in America in our own image; a place to go other than home or work. We also created an industry that did not exist: specialty coffee."[13] Schultz followed an aggressive expansion and partnership strategy to grow the company. Over time, Starbucks's success to a large extent depended on its ability to partner and tap into the innovation of other providers and suppliers. The success of Starbucks's alliances came about as a result of Schultz's personal involvement in making them work.

Starbucks used alliances in four areas to drive innovation:

1. Discovering, sourcing, and marketing specialty coffees, teas, and foods from different parts of the world. Starbucks's coffee buyers travel to farms in Latin America, Africa, and Asia to select the highest-quality coffee beans. They want their supplier base to grow and support Starbucks's growth. It is not widely known that Starbucks participates in Fair Trade, the social movement to help producers in developing countries obtain better conditions. Fair Trade pays locally owned coffee plantations top dollar for high-quality beans. It ensures a sustainable supply of coffee to support Starbucks's growing business.

2. Developing and marketing products that suit the unique and evolving taste of consumers. Starbucks's deal with bookseller Barnes & Noble to create small coffee shops in their stores was highly successful and led to deals with

other retailers. Another example of this success with other companies was the Frappuccino. Starbucks tied up with PepsiCo to sell a bottled version of Frappuccino in retail stores and vending machines. In 2015, Starbucks signed another deal with PepsiCo to market and distribute Starbucks products in several Latin American countries. Another notable strategic alliance was made in 2011 with Tata Coffee, Asia's largest coffee plantation company, to bring Starbucks to India. The venture allowed Starbucks to market Indian-blended coffee in global markets.

3. Enhancing the customer experience. Starbucks formed a partnership with Yahoo to provide digital networks in its stores. Yahoo delivered premium content sites such as *USA Today*, *Wall Street Journal*, *ESPN*, and others when a customer connected through Starbucks's free Wi-Fi. Starbucks also agreed to a partnership with Apple to collaborate on selling music as part of the "coffee house experience."

4. Creating a workspace where Starbucks baristas, the employees who serve customers, feel valued and appreciated. Starbucks partnered with Arizona State University in 2014 to offer U.S. Starbucks employees tuition assistance, to help them earn college degrees.

Starbucks has opened an average of two new stores every day since 1987.[14] It is now the largest coffeehouse company in the world, with 20,891 stores in 62 countries, including 13,279 in the United States. In 2012, *Forbes* magazine ranked Schultz's net worth at $1.5 billion.

Partnerships or strategic alliances are an alternate approach to boosting innovation in-house or through acquisitions. According to a report by the Chief Marketing Officer Council, 85% of respondents to a survey viewed partnerships and alliances as essential or important to their businesses.[15] Some 44% seek alliances for new ideas, insights, and innovation, while 57% said they use partnerships to acquire customers. Even when companies form partnerships, they do not always know how to make them work. An estimated 60% of alliances fail due to lack of governance—for example, day-to-day management.

Companies often staff alliance organizations with members of their own sales team. Members of the sourcing staff are frequently not considered or thought capable of managing alliances. But alliance partners are not customers, and the sales tool kits for customer management are not appropriate for them.

Alliance relationships are similar to supplier relationships, intertwined but at arm's length. Sourcing organizations have experience with deal negotiations and governance of these types of relationships. Unfortunately, most CEOs are not aware of the sourcing organization's capabilities and instead involve sales or business teams in leading and finalizing their strategic alliances. Very little attention is given to making the deal operational, and this oversight often leads to a failure of the alliance. Involving the sourcing organization in deal negotiations and in the governance or ongoing partner engagement can significantly improve the success of the alliance.

NOKIA'S FAILURE TO EMBRACE ALLIANCES

Failing to form and nurture partnerships can be fatal. Take, for example, Nokia's struggle in the wireless handset market. The company had two lines of business: telecommunication network products and wireless handsets. The world's first mobile phone (GSM) call was made by the Finnish prime minister in 1991 using Nokia equipment.

By 1998, Nokia overtook Motorola, becoming the bestselling mobile phone brand. Though Nokia was not that popular in the United States, it was incredibly successful in Europe, Africa, Asia, and Oceania. Nokia pioneered mobile gaming and launched the first camera phone in the North American market. Nokia's Symbian operating system was the leading smartphone platform in Europe and Asia.

In the early 2000s, wireless operators such as Vodafone, T-Mobile, NTT DOCOMO, Verizon, AT&T, and others were investing heavily to launch 3G services to provide email and the Internet to customers. Three different services were converging—mobile, broadcasting, and computing. Wireless operators were looking to partner with handset manufacturers to define and introduce these new data services. At the same time, handsets were expected to go through a radical change, and Nokia's traditional competitive advantage came under threat. Miniaturization and style were losing out to consumers' need for smartphones, phones that are capable of connecting with the web and providing rich content.

With the 9210 Communicator, which had a tiny keyboard concealed in a thick handset, Nokia had a working model of a smartphone, and operators were looking to partner with them. This was six years before Apple's iPhone was launched.

Our team was hired by Nokia's U.S. marketing leader to help define its data strategy. Our analysis showed that Nokia would have a difficult time winning in the market if it did not partner with wireless operators. Nokia's team agreed with our recommendations but didn't relay these findings to their Finnish leadership team. They were concerned that our strategy contradicted corporate strategy.

The leadership team continued to believe that its power to define the wireless ecosystem lay in Nokia's selling directly to consumers. Nokia refused to partner with wireless operators and provide any exclusivity to them. In the United States, Samsung tied up with Verizon, and LG partnered with both Verizon and AT&T.

In 2007, Apple launched the iPhone in partnership with AT&T and agreed to provide the carrier with five years of exclusivity. The partnership benefited both companies. The AT&T user base and the revenue per user grew exponentially, and Apple became the dominant smartphone manufacturer. The introduction of the iPhone not only negatively impacted Nokia but also Motorola, BlackBerry, Sony, and others.

Nokia failed to introduce smartphones that could effectively compete with iPhones and ended up focusing on selling in developing countries. It eventually sold its mobile phone business to Microsoft in 2013. Nokia's CEO, Stephen Elop, delivered an elegy for the company's mobile phone business, ending it by saying, "We did not do anything wrong, but somehow, we lost."

Nokia failed for many reasons—leadership issues, the inability to innovate, investing in the wrong technology, and others. I believe Nokia failed primarily due to the company's refusal to partner with wireless operators, which hampered its ability to innovate with smartphones. Microsoft struggled with the Nokia acquisition and in 2015 wrote off $7.6 billion, nearly the entire price it paid for Nokia.

SOURCING'S INVOLVEMENT IN ALLIANCES

This and other kinds of alliance-related disasters can be avoided by getting the sourcing organization involved early on in the decision-making process. Should an alliance be formed? If so, with whom? And how should it be governed?

At a leading biotech company, a sourcing leader was asked to head the alliance organization. He was known for his ability to work with suppliers and make difficult supplier engagements work. The company saw value in his ability to streamline engagement with alliance partners.

The executive soon identified and fixed two problems with the company's existing approach. First, it was using old, combative negotiation techniques to work with its alliance partners, rather than a modern, collaborative approach. As a result, the process lacked transparency and reduced trust between the parties. Second, a governance structure was missing. The lack of any alignment of goals, metrics, and tracking mechanisms led to constant recrimination and finger-pointing.

Sourcing organizations can help solve these problems in several ways.

Transparent Deal Negotiation

Traditional negotiation strategies depend on not sharing information with strategic partners. The relationship starts with mutual distrust and a feeling that the other party is there to take advantage of the relationship. An approach like this quickly unravels into a combative discussion and undermines any trust between the parties.

A better approach is to be transparent during the deal negotiations and create a flexible framework that can be used to renegotiate the terms as circumstances change. As an example, one of the tools we have successfully used is "should-cost" modeling. The objective of the should-cost model is to identify underlying economic drivers. Sometimes there is confusion about the difference between actual cost and should-cost. The difference may stem from past decisions that may have resulted in excess investments, processes not laid out in an optimal way, or some other factors. Most of the time the difference between should-cost and actual cost is not big and doesn't significantly impact the negotiations. However, if the differences are significant, then we call it out in the model. These differences are considered during negotiations when appropriate.

Sourcing organizations develop cost models for specific requirements. Developing a cost-modeling tool kit becomes critical for alliance deal negotiations because understanding the underlying costs can help to identify opportunities for outcome improvements. This concept is sometimes confusing to our clients because they think the sole objective of cost modeling is to reduce costs, and they do not understand the linkage between cost and the improvement of outcome or service. Cost modeling is a tool that can also identify areas where costs could be added or redirected so as to improve service or the quality of the product in addition to making the operation more efficient. The level of sophistication and collaboration required for should-cost modeling for alliances is far greater, as it requires a deeper level of trust from both parties that such information will be used in a constructive fashion.

We have used should-cost models across many different industries and corporations where we readily shared the information with alliance partners. We also allowed partners to provide feedback and input to the model. It became a living document that provided insight into the economic drivers of the deal and a template for future negotiations.

Sometimes people who create a model try to manipulate it to serve their own organization's objectives. They do so, for example, by using their own proprietary data. To avoid any such appearance of bias, we use only third-party data, whether to validate assumptions or as inputs to the model. This ensures transparency and creates mutual trust.

The following illustration provides an example of should-cost modeling and the value it can bring to structuring deals: A specialized call center contract at a pharmaceutical company specified that the provider maintain infrastructure at a particular location with a set of stringent technical requirements. The conditions changed significantly over time due to the changing business environment. However, both companies struggled to figure out how best to restructure their relationship. A should-cost modeling effort showed significant potential for service improvement by spending more on representatives who answer calls and less on overhead areas such as program management and administration. Also, it showed an opportunity to reduce technology cost by using off-the-shelf technology. After the model was implemented, overall costs came down by 25%. The change in contract structure provided flexibility to the partner in determining which infrastructure would be used in various locations.

Another example relates to a wholesaler agreement for a pharmaceutical company. The company, which considered wholesalers as partners, relied on them to distribute their products to hospitals, clinics, and doctor offices.

The company believed that wholesalers could increase its revenue and considered these relationships strategic. The company was launching a new drug and entering a new market. Its relationship with wholesalers was contentious, and wholesalers were pushing back on the prices sought by the company. Traditional negotiation approaches were not working because the company lacked a clear understanding of the concerns raised by wholesalers.

Our firm was asked to develop a should-cost model to identify the underlying economic drivers and then use these findings to bring about transparent negotiations with the wholesalers, who included McKesson, AmerisourceBergen, and others. Such wholesalers make money by charging a distribution fee and a quick payment fee, both of these determined as a percentage (typically 2% to 5%) of the pharmaceutical product price. The wholesalers' primary cost was the physical transportation of the products from customers to the hospital or doctor's office. The products came in different sizes—single-pack, six-pack, or ten-pack. The distribution cost did not vary much whether a product was delivered in ten-pack sizes or single packs. But wholesalers' revenues did vary with pack size since they were determined by the pharmaceutical product price. Wholesalers made more money on ten-packs than on singles. In the case of this new product introduction, wholesalers were being asked to distribute a disproportionate number of singles. That, by definition, made the job unattractive to them. Hence, their pushback.

Our team relied on three sources of nonproprietary data to create the model: public financial information, proxy data for customer segment and SLAs, and actual pricing data for distribution cost drivers. Customer service–level agreements include, among other things, inventory holdings, delivery frequency, and billing agreements. The model was shared with wholesalers to ensure our assumptions were correct.

The analysis showed that wholesalers were earning, overall, a higher margin from this customer than they were from other pharmaceutical clients. The problem stemmed entirely from the new product introduction, where the company's emphasis on delivering a high number of lower-priced single packs stood to reduce wholesalers' profit. In fact, wholesalers would make negative margins on such deliveries. Figure 3.1 shows the wholesaler profitability for different pack sizes.

To address the concerns with single packs, our team suggested that the company consider an alternate distribution structure by splitting the wholesalers' customer management function from the physical

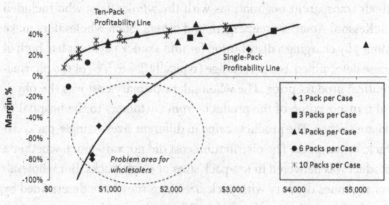

Figure 3.1—Wholesaler Profitability by Pack Size

distribution of product. Wholesalers were known for their customer management—order processing and inventory management—and it probably made sense to use their expertise in that area.

The biggest cost to wholesalers was transportation; it made sense, for this product introduction, to assign the job of distribution to UPS or FedEx rather than the wholesalers. We also suggested that the customer renegotiate its wholesaler agreement to align it better with the firm's corporate objectives. The proposed changes included changing wholesaler compensation as dollar per unit instead of percentage of pharmaceutical price. Also, we recommended using wholesalers based on their geographic strength and implemented a partner engagement model designed to help resolve compensation and other issues up front.

Partner Engagement: Ongoing Relationship Management

Most companies' relationships with their alliance partners are somewhat adversarial. There is a mentality that the needs of alliance partners are subservient to the needs of the corporation. In this thinking, partners should provide the service while companies are clients who pay for the service. This policy lacks a collaborative approach that would enable both the company and the partner to focus on the same goal. Imagine if this kind of thinking ruled your relationship with a significant other: How long would that last?

Why does this happen? In some cases, there is a mismatch in incentives. Line management is incentivized to get the work done, not for their ability to collaborate with external parties. It is important for leadership to understand that the business environment is changing, and that the ability or inability to work with partners can lead to success or failure in the marketplace.

Developing a collaborative approach begins with accepting the fact that partners bring value to the table. This is why companies decide to work with them in the first place. They are capable of delivering excellent outcomes in their particular area of expertise. The objective of partner engagement should be to enable partners while holding them accountable for doing their job well. If partners do not perform consistently, then a company should disengage. But it should also resist the urge to micromanage partners' actions.

Below are a few steps that have helped companies get more from their alliances by improving partner engagement.

STEP 1—CLEARLY DEFINE BUSINESS GOALS

Most companies lack a good way of setting expectations with partners. For any relationship to work, expectation setting is critical. Yet the practice of using SLAs to state what is expected is not widely followed. Functional management has a difficult time articulating what services they need from their partners. When SLAs are used, they often do not link back to the business objectives the company is hoping to achieve and instead focus on tasks performed by the partner.

For example, many contracts for outsourced janitorial services focus on the frequency of cleaning, rather than on customer satisfaction with cleanliness. If a janitorial firm cleaned at the frequency agreed to in the contract but did not achieve customer satisfaction with cleanliness, then the SLAs were not tying back to the right goal.

It is essential to think beyond the obvious service or product that a partner is providing and understand the business goals to get better value from partner engagement. For example, one of our financial services clients provided free bus service to its employees to transport them from New York City to the client's offices in nearby Connecticut.

Here, the business goal was more than just providing transportation. It was to incentivize employees to make the trip every day and to ensure that they were productive en route. The service was meant to be both recruitment and a retention tool. A well-crafted SLA would state that the transportation provider would have to be able to address these higher needs, in addition to providing safe bus rides.

STEP 2—TIE METRICS TO BUSINESS GOALS

There is usually confusion about the difference between SLAs and key performance indicators (KPIs). The way I like to explain the concept is that SLAs are a simple way of defining your needs, and KPIs are the metrics that help you measure how well your needs are being met. For example: In order to provide great transportation service to the financial services client, an SLA for the transportation provider would ask for drivers who excelled at customer service in addition to safe driving. To measure how well the transportation provider was doing in this respect, KPIs would include employee feedback on driver conduct, how well drivers kept employees informed during the trip, and the drivers' helpfulness and friendliness. These metrics would be needed just as much as a driver's motoring history and accident record.

STEP 3—THINK BUSINESS OUTCOME BEFORE COST

In companies where alliance management programs had been implemented, we found the overwhelming focus was on cost, not on business outcomes. Depending on the alliance's goals, the business outcome could be revenue growth, market penetration, or something else. Most partners are chosen for their ability to perform a job better than the internal organizations. So why is there such a focus on cost? The role played by business organizations in setting up these programs is minimal. The contracts are mostly designed by finance organizations without business organization involvement. If you do not measure business outcomes, how will you know if the partner is performing well? You know the old saying "What gets measured gets delivered." There is a need to review the metrics to ensure partners are focused on the right goals.

STEP 4—PROVIDE BOTH INCENTIVES AND PENALTIES

We found that most contracts do not have any incentives or penalties associated with the levels of service provided. Some set penalties but provide no incentive for good performance. It is well known that positive reinforcement works better than negative reinforcement. Ask anyone who has steered their children in the right direction.

So why do most contracts contain penalties for nonperformance but few to no incentives for performing above and beyond expectations? The view of contract teams seems to be that partners are incentivized enough when a company provides them with additional business. That may be true. However, behavioral scientists will tell you that direct incentives work better than indirect ones. Further, incentives and penalties do not have to be material. Even a small financial reward like 1% to 2% of total contract value may be enough to incentivize partners to contribute their best effort.

A system of incentives will help you recognize what the partner needs to improve and what it is doing well. Providing a mixture of small monetary benefits and penalties ensures attention from the leadership of both companies to these metrics. However, it is critical that these incentives and penalties are not big, as there is a risk of taking partner focus away from the work at hand. Also, I like to provide incentives for a softer measure, such as customer service feedback, and penalties for such harder measures as timeliness, quality, and delivery, which are more under the partner's control.

STEP 5—USE FACT/DATA-BASED PERFORMANCE MEASUREMENT INSTEAD OF PERCEPTION

Opinions are easy to get; facts and data less so. Engagement works better if it is based on facts and data, not swayed by subjective perceptions. Facts and data allow partners to focus on tasks and have productive discussions without arousing emotions. Also, it becomes easier to identify trends and to determine whether performance is improving or not. I sometimes get pushback about our focus on facts because managers feel that not everything can be captured with data. This may be true, but thinking through the right KPIs can help in devising good methods for data capture. It could be surveys or feedback on performance from key stakeholders at certain milestones. It helps to be transparent with partners on when and how data will be captured, so there is no question about how their performance will be measured.

STEP 6—ENCOURAGE TWO-WAY FEEDBACK

Typically, most discussions with partners focus on providing them with feedback about their performance and the areas in which they could improve. We all know companies can also do things on their end that can help improve the overall results. To our surprise, many managers who have been involved in this type of discussion did not actively ask partners for feedback. The partners were also reluctant to provide the information for fear of alienating the other party. It was a missed opportunity on both sides to collaborate better. I have received excellent ideas from partners about possible improvements. Partners are closer to the work. Missing out on the opportunity to get partner feedback is just plain unwise.

STEP 7—ESTABLISH A REGULAR CADENCE FOR PERFORMANCE REVIEW

Setting up a regular schedule to measure and communicate partner performance is always a good idea. This avoids surprises and allows time to fix any issues. The biggest benefit is that partners understand that someone is reviewing their performance and transmitting it to their stakeholders. This is the best way to hold partners and internal organizations accountable.

Most programs for engaging partners and managing partner relationships are tactical and punitive in nature and don't help in building long-term relationships. A well-thought-out design for a partner engagement model allows companies to drive better business results and get greater value from their alliance partners. A greater effort to find common objectives and innovative solutions with partners can help to achieve long-term profitability and success for both parties.

MAKING ALLIANCES SUCCESSFUL WITH SOURCING

Alliances continue to play a significant role in business success. A well-executed alliance can propel companies toward an agreed-upon objective, which each would find difficult to attain on its own. Many well-planned alliances fail because executives take their eyes off the ball after an agreement has been reached and fail to make the deal operational. In other words, lack of governance or day-to-day management leads to conflict that ultimately leads to alliance failure.

CEOs typically rely on sales teams to make their deals operational. Unfortunately, alliance or partner management is not one of the sales team's core competencies. It's part of the sourcing tool kit. Sourcing organizations are involved in striking deals with suppliers and then making them operational. Many of their tools could be modified to make alliances successful.

What does this mean for the sourcing organization? We've helped a number of companies set up successful alliance relationships, and here are some best practices we found useful in implementing them, no matter what the size:

- The sourcing organization should be asked to contribute directly to business strategy, moving from being a cost center to becoming an integral part of the business similar to the marketing or R&D departments. A sourcing team's contribution to business strategy will come by developing and managing strategic partners who can drive business outcomes such as increased revenue and reduced risks or reduced cost at a corporate level. Based on their involvement with an organization they might be referred to as innovation partners, outsourcing partners, contract manufacturers, wholesalers, or sales and service partners. Sourcing organizations already have supplier relationship management programs for different suppliers, and extending the program to alliance partners would not be difficult.
- Sourcing organizations will have to change their approach to managing strategic partners. I have seen firsthand several examples where chief procurement officers came to recognize strategic suppliers as an area of opportunity but lacked the necessary tools and skills in their organizations to successfully engage these providers.
- Working with strategic partners requires two key skill sets: a collaborative mindset and an analytics-based approach. This is a different approach from the method currently used for category management, where the market or competitive forces drive efficiency. Persuasion and influencing skills can be more important than ability to negotiate pricing or contracts with suppliers. Also, managing partners from arm's length with transparency to operations becomes critical. A robust partner management process is required.

In the next chapter, we will switch gears and talk about how the supply chain and sourcing organization can help with managing overall corporate risk, not just risk in their respective sphere of control. As technology is disrupting industries, corporate risk management becomes critical for long-term survival of companies. Look at the bankruptcies and liquidation among brick-and-mortar retailers. Supply chain and sourcing can help companies survive when they face headwind in their business by removing bottlenecks and managing overheads.

PART

REDUCE BUSINESS RISK THROUGH EFFICIENT OPERATIONS

4

DEBOTTLENECK THE SUPPLY CHAIN AND REDUCE RISK

BUSINESS RISKS FROM SUPPLY CHAIN

Apple and Supply Chain

Soon after he returned to Apple as CEO in 1997, Steve Jobs focused his talent on three problem areas: Apple's product pipeline, its marketing, and its supply chain.[16]

Why would a creative person like Jobs waste his time on the supply chain? He worried that Apple was not keeping up with innovations in distribution and inventory management. At that time, Apple had two to three months of supplier inventory and another two to three months of finished goods inventory. The concept is similar to planes lining up to taxi at an airport. The plane that just left the gate has to wait for planes that are taxiing ahead. Similarly, unless the older inventory sells, the new product from Apple factories cannot reach customers.

Unbelievable as it may seem with the sleek organization Apple deploys today, the company then had to guess four to six months in advance about customer demand. Jobs claimed that "we are not smart enough to do that; [even] I am not smart enough to do that."

Jobs removed inventory from the pipeline. In his mind, this would allow customers to tell Apple what they wanted, and Apple could then respond to their needs extremely quickly.

To push supply chain innovation, Jobs hired Tim Cook from Compaq in 1998 as head of Apple's worldwide operations. Cook was quoted as saying: "You want to manage it like you're in the dairy business. If it gets past its freshness date, you have a problem."[17]

Cook closed factories and warehouses, replacing them with contract manufacturers, causing a reduction in the company's inventory from months to days by reducing the time from factory to customers. It is like closing down the taxi runway and using the extra space to fly or land airplanes.

Cook also made strategic long-term investments in key components such as flash memory, guaranteeing a stable supply of what would become an essential component for the iPod nano, and later the iPhone and the iPad. Apple competitors struggled to get supplies as Apple locked up all the manufacturing capacity for those components, creating an advantage for Apple.

Cook's efforts to improve Apple's supply chain were credited with helping the company achieve financial success, along with Jobs's design and marketing savvy. Cook was promoted to COO in 2007, and then to CEO in August 2011 when he succeeded Jobs.

The supply chain in too many companies becomes a bottleneck—a garden hose so leaky that only a trickle of water emerges from its nozzle. As you fix one leak, water pours from another. The whole organization spends so much time applying patches that it doesn't have time to think about the future. The way to fix the problem permanently is to simplify customer engagement, the planning processes, and communication with suppliers.

Benefits of Debottlenecking Supply Chain

Let's first look at a classic bottleneck example. A leading U.S. consumer goods company entered the Indian market by acquiring a pharmaceutical company and then expanding its presence to consumer products such as detergent, shampoo, and others. The acquired firm, which specialized in over-the-counter drugs, faced entrenched local competition. Local rivals started launching brands to preempt every potential product launch by the U.S. parent. Trying to fight back, the Indian company discovered that its supply chain had become a sales bottleneck.

The lead time to launch a new product in India was several months to a year. The average inventory was 120 days old, with significant nonmoving inventory clogging the system. Despite having so much inventory, in many places the company was running out of stock because a large percentage of the firm's products were at the wrong locations.

As a result, the supply chain organization was constantly paying to expedite shipments from one location to another. While management concentrated on putting out fires, the company steadily lost market share. When the parent company became alarmed, the Indian CEO called in special talent to help identify the root causes of the problem.

The team soon identified one source: the sales tactic known as "stuffing the channel"—an artificial way of making financial numbers look good without anything ever having been sold. The company's sales team, to meet its targets, was forcing products that hadn't been ordered onto distributors who, in turn, were forcing them onto retailers.

The practice clogged the company's distribution system. Both distributors and retailers became upset with the company's practices and started refusing to accept any new products. It took several months for the inventory to be sold, and some products languished in the firm's warehouses because there was no demand for them. Over time, the pile of nonmoving inventory grew like cancer, and there was no money to support new product launches.

Channel stuffing is not unique to this company or to India. It routinely happens, for example, in the U.S. automobile industry, where inventory is pushed to dealers. The downturn in the car industry in 2008 was exacerbated by sales channel stuffing and repeated sales promotions.

Back in India, the drug company took several steps to do what I call "debottlenecking" its supply chain.

The first step was to survey the network being used to get goods and materials from suppliers to manufacturing plants, then finished goods to consumers. There were 24 plants, 30 warehouses, and 2,400 depots spread across the country. Depots were small warehouses maintained outside major metropolitan areas to service distributors and small retailers in outlying areas. Many depot locations were found to be redundant. How much inventory was gathering dust in them? No one seemed to know. A complete overhaul of the supply chain was proposed.

Once the survey was complete, the company began improving its warehouse and transit procedures to get a proper understanding of the size and location of its inventory.

A strict system of accounting was implemented in each warehouse and depot, which increased inventory accuracy from 75% to 99% (meaning that 99% of the time the inventory in the warehouse matched what was on the books). The team improved visibility to transit inventory by keeping better track of dispatch between warehouses and depots. They further linked the system in the depots to the main office, making inventory information available to the CEO and the planning team 24/7 in real time.

The third step was to reduce inventory and get rid of nonmoving goods. The company scrapped most of the nonmoving inventory. This took courage from the CEO because it involved taking a significant financial hit. As inventory was reduced, several deficiencies in the supply chain became evident, such as the long lead time required to deliver to some depots.

Management then used computer modeling to optimize the flow of goods and determine inventory levels at different stock points. The team implemented several recommendations that were a radical break from past practice. They consolidated 24 plants to just 2 and reduced 2,400 depots to 30. They also relocated warehouses next to manufacturing plants. This enabled the company to respond faster to market demand and helped bring about a significant inventory reduction.

The average time inventory spent in warehouses was reduced from 115 days to 75 days. The team realized that the inventory levels were also dependent on the fluctuation of supply and demand. The main culprit was the sales promotions run by the company to push the stock to distributors and retailers at the month's end. Sales promotions were part of the former channel-stuffing program and had little or no impact on actual sales to consumers. It was difficult to predict how much inventory would be required to meet the end-of-month push.

Management was able to reduce supply-and-demand fluctuations by increasing the reliability of the transportation network, by abolishing useless sales promotions, and by eliminating stuffing. This reform also required courage on the part of the CEO, because the firm knew revenue would fall for several quarters as retail stocks were reduced. To improve transportation, the team decided to work only with firms that had a good track record for reliability, even if that meant paying a premium price.

The last step was to get rid of forecasts, using demand instead to pull products from the factory. In the past, despite their best efforts, product forecasts had been unreliable. With improved communication, demand information became readily available. The company decided that it would only pull products from warehouses after orders were received, which in turn initiated a demand from the factory. It was a complete and radical departure from the push mindset. This change was also difficult for management, as it meant sometimes keeping plants idle when the products were not selling. However, it allowed plants to retool for products that were more popular and had better sales figures. The motto became:

"Don't produce if it is not selling."

The results of all of these efforts were impressive: The company regained its market initiative and began launching products every month, with new products contributing 50% to 70% of next year's sales. Market share improved. And the productivity of the sales team rose by 30% to 50% as it focused more on selling than pushing products to distributors and retailers. Operationally, the cost of delivery declined from 75% of the sales price to 55%.

System inventory shrank from 115 days to 60 days. Perfect orders—meaning orders where the right quantity is delivered at the right time, with the right billing—rose from 40% to 90%. At the same time, quality, as measured by the defect rate per million items produced, improved from 30,000 to 5,000. Products were fresher when they reached consumers, whose satisfaction with the company's product naturally increased. Retailers and distributors were happy to work with the company again. Eventually, India became the health care manufacturing center for the U.S. firm's worldwide operations.

Bottom line?

The company made twice as much money for the same product after debottlenecking its supply chain.

How was that possible?

When you reduce inventory, you start taking cost out of the system. Transportation is more efficient, with a higher percentage of shipments being dispatched in full truckloads. Container utilization (the percentage of a container filled) increases. Factories are better able to streamline their processes, meaning rejected items are reduced.

Last—but definitely not least—people simply do a better job when they do not have to rush from one task to another plugging leaks.

So, if all this is true, why do so many great companies still tolerate bad supply chains? A friend of mine, who heads the supply chain organization at a global tech company, explains some of the reasons. After years of adding new products, customers, and suppliers, a company's supply chain eventually becomes unmanageable. There are too many decision makers—planners, manufacturing teams, and the procurement organization. They are all driven by their individual needs and objectives, and there is no single point of accountability. As my friend put it, "Too many cooks spoil the broth," and there is rarely a consensus on how to proceed.

Among the issues faced by many companies is the inventory planning system, which may not function optimally because there is too much variability. The IT system that was implemented to produce the inventory reports may be a few years old and unable to deal with new changes. Each report, which is designed to help with the decision-making process, may now take hours to run, and each time you want to make a change you have to start afresh. Companies try to employ big data solutions to make sense of the massive amounts of data being accumulated every day, but the quality of the data is suspect, or the logic of the proposed solution is not sound. What do you think is happening at the customer end? I am sure they are frustrated or worse and may be looking for a replacement supplier.

SUPPLY CHAIN CHALLENGES AT THE DEPARTMENT OF DEFENSE (DOD)

This problem is not unique to the commercial world. Consider the reports of the U.S. Government Accountability Office (GAO). It has been telling Congress that the DOD supply chain management is a "high-risk area due in part to ineffective and inefficient inventory-management practices."[18] This defense bottleneck is a direct result of the supply chain's complexity.

We are talking here about hundreds of billions of dollars in excess inventory, with huge back orders. Plainly stated, the government has too much inventory that it does not need and too little of the things it requires to fight wars, resulting in several billion dollars' worth of losses to taxpayers every year. More significantly, these shortcomings compromise military readiness.

Napoleon lost his war against Russia in 1812 because his armies could not be supplied with food and warm clothing in Russia's harsh winter climate. Similarly, during World War II, Germany struggled unsuccessfully to supply its forces in Russia. In North Africa, it lost out to better-supplied Allied units, because the Allies dominated shipping in the Mediterranean.

SUPPLY CHAIN COMPLEXITY

I'll explain the generic problem of complexity in Figure 4.1, which is an example of an over-the-counter pharmaceutical product supply chain that spans three continents.

Figure 4.1—Supply Chain for an Over-the-Counter Pharmaceutical Product

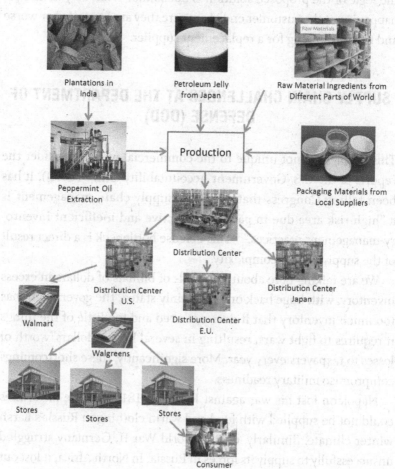

Plantations in India

Petroleum Jelly from Japan

Raw Material Ingredients from Different Parts of World

Production

Peppermint Oil Extraction

Packaging Materials from Local Suppliers

Distribution Center

Distribution Center U.S.

Distribution Center Japan

Walmart

Distribution Center E.U.

Walgreens

Stores

Stores

Stores

Consumer

Vicks VapoRub—a simple over-the-counter pharmaceutical product manufactured in India by Procter & Gamble—requires peppermint oil extracted from menthol plants grown in India. The oil gets combined at a factory in India with petroleum jelly made in Japan. It then travels through the supply chain across continents to reach consumers in the United States and Europe, where it can be found in any pharmacy.

Peppermint oil is sold in various sizes (1 liter, 10 liters, and 50 liters), as is every other raw and packing material that goes into Va-poRub. Each country has its own requirement on sizes for the product. Developing countries prefer smaller packaging because of consumer affordability issues, and developed countries prefer larger containers. Even for such a simple product, the supply chain can become incredibly complex. Figure 4.1 shows how the multiple handoffs in a supply chain can drive complexity.

Unfortunately, many CEOs, corporate executives, and government leaders do not understand supply chains. To fix the supply chain problem, they usually resort to changing leadership and selecting leaders from manufacturing, IT, sourcing, or finance organizations. They also do not understand how the operation works and sometimes get caught in the "deer in the headlights" syndrome—a complete paralysis. In other cases, they simply avoid the problem and hope it gets resolved on its own.

Another solution that is commonly entertained is simply outsourcing the supply chain. FedEx, UPS, and other suppliers have made big business out of this. Though outsourcing for parts of the supply chain may help, operational problems need to be fixed whether managed in-house or by an outsourced provider. Even when companies hire the right talent to lead the supply chain, they have to solve operational processing problems first. This requires a methodical and step-by-step approach.

As Jobs always said, the way to debottleneck a problem is to simplify, simplify, simplify. The following approaches have worked for my clients.

REDUCING NONMOVING INVENTORY

For many companies, a significant portion of their inventory is non-moving. No one is ordering those products, but they occupy valuable warehouse space and clog the system. It is estimated that more than 90% of the Defense Logistics Agency's[19] inventory is either nonmoving, meaning it had not been ordered in the last five years, or it is slow moving, meaning it has not been ordered in a year. Imagine what happens when a significant portion of the available storage space is occupied by inventory that doesn't move and that keeps increasing every day.

Nonmoving inventory not only occupies valuable warehouse space but also represents locked-up cash that is not available for revenue generation. This could mean a decreased ability to launch new products, make investments in R&D, or upgrade manufacturing. Also, it costs money to borrow cash for inventory that no one is buying.

It is not hard for companies to free themselves from this nonmoving inventory. Retailers do it all the time: giving discounts or even taking substantial markdowns for clearance items. They sell these items at a loss, but not a 100% loss. Unfortunately, this luxury is not always available to all companies. For many companies, products have a shelf life, and once a product expires they have to scrap the inventory. Scrapping of nonmoving inventory reflects poorly on profit columns. Cisco wrote off a $2.2 billion inventory in 2001. On April 6, 2001, Cisco's stock sank to $13.63 from $82, which it had reached 13 months earlier.

In the DOD's case, such a big agency does not always know when nonmoving inventory will be suddenly required for a product that has long been discontinued by its suppliers, such as an engine part for a helicopter that has been in service for many years. This runs the risk of critical assets not functioning due to lack of spare parts on hand.

Scrapping nonmoving inventory is probably the best approach for recognizing the true value of inventory in the commercial world. If scrapping is not possible, inventory should be moved out of the regular supply chain's warehousing and held at an offsite location. This will make room for goods that are selling. At the same time, there is a screaming need to stop piling up nonmoving inventory. This can be accomplished by analyzing the reasons for the nonmoving inventory buildup and then developing strategies to address them.

SIMPLIFYING ORDERING

With the advent of mobile technology and the Internet, customers can order products through multiple channels. There are two ways to manage customer orders—assisted ordering and self-help. Assisted ordering is when a customer phones a call center or visits a retail site to order products or services. Self-help is when a customer orders the product through the Internet, a mobile device, or a catalog. In terms of cost, retail is the most expensive, followed by call centers, and then self-help, which is the cheapest. What is not commonly known is that ordering errors are far less common with self-help than assisted ordering. Error rates increase with multiple people handling documents. Ordering errors can create a significant problem for the supply chain, as it results in increased customer returns. So why do companies still prefer to have retail sites? It allows them to cross-sell or up-sell products to customers visiting the store.

The use of retail sites pervades federal agencies as well. The DLA (Defense Logistics Agency) and GSS (General Supply Services), which are logistics agencies that govern purchases by federal agencies, have retail sites at other federal agencies such as Veterans Affairs or the Department of State. The logic of having these locations is to help federal employees make knowledgeable decisions by having supplier representatives explain the products to them. Some of these retail locations barely get any traffic, but both of these agencies spend huge sums to operate them. In the federal world, it is hard to close any site due to political involvement, so simplifying the ordering process is not simple.

STREAMLINING THE SUPPLY CHAIN

Simplifying the supply chain and having a separate supply chain for different types of demand profiles can significantly reduce the clutter. Simplification could involve removing warehouses and simplifying

Figure 4.2—Defense Logistics Agency Supply Chain: Current vs. Proposed

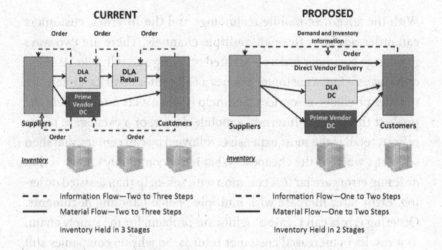

- - - Information Flow—Two to Three Steps
——— Material Flow—Two to Three Steps
Inventory Held in 3 Stages

- - - Information Flow—One to Two Steps
——— Material Flow—One to Two Steps
Inventory Held in 2 Stages

the material flow in warehouses. Separating supply chain could mean having a different supply chain for fast-moving, slow-moving, and non-moving products. Depending on the type of product and its demand pattern, separation can happen at the manufacturing or supplier end. Figure 4.2 is a suggested improvement for streamlining the DLA supply chain. Which one do you think makes delivery to customers easier? The one that requires fewer steps from suppliers to customers, that is, the proposed solution.

SIMPLIFYING DELIVERY

The last mile of the supply chain—the delivery to customers—is probably the most expensive. When Amazon ships, for example, it cannot combine your shipment with that of your neighbor. Your neighbor may have ordered different products and may have a different delivery date. You will not be happy if Amazon tells you that your shipment is delayed because of your neighbor's order.

Companies employ multiple delivery methods to replenish customer demand. The likelihood of error increases rapidly as more steps are involved in the delivery process. It probably makes sense to deliver fast-moving products directly to the customer from the factory or from the vendor if manufacturing is outsourced.

Of course, you have to consider the order size and cost of shipment while making the choice. The cost of shipment may increase, but direct deliveries from the plant have shown to be cheaper for large order sizes because they remove interim handling and storage costs. Many companies are colocating their distribution centers with a manufacturing site to make this happen.

For slow-moving items, it makes sense to consolidate shipments and then ship to customers. Once direct delivery from the factory has been implemented, it makes sense to review the network and adjust the footprint of different warehouses. It may mean removing some, adding space, or removing space in others.

Let's take the example of the automotive delivery model. We traditionally buy a car from a local dealer. It is one of the most painful and dreaded experiences most consumers have endured. However, it continues to be the dominant delivery model for the automotive industry. If you think about it, this delivery model is a type of assisted retail.

Consumers need to test-drive cars to see what they would like to buy and need help in deciding the right configuration. However, is it necessary to deliver cars through dealers? Not really. If consumers are comfortable receiving computers directly from manufacturers, they will probably not be resistant to receiving cars directly to their home.

Dealers can continue to play the role of showcasing different products and providing servicing. Car companies could capture an order and directly deliver to customers by combining shipments within a city or neighborhood. This would reduce inventory, lower costs, and improve product choices for consumers. Some work on the transportation network would be required, but the infrastructure already exists and could be outsourced.

Why has this not been tried? The electric car company Tesla, founded by maverick businessman Elon Musk, has actually introduced sales without dealers, but it has run into opposition from dealers. The state of New Jersey even banned Tesla sales because of this dealerless model thanks to the political support dealers receive at the state level.

SIMPLIFYING PLANNING

Most companies plan shipment for a product or service by using demand forecasts based on historical data. However, forecast accuracy tends to be low, sometimes below 50%. The odds are similar to flipping a coin. Shipments based on forecasts result in inventory being dispatched to the wrong places. It is better to use real-time data to determine shipping. The information is likely to be more accurate, and inventory will reach the places where it is needed most.

A typical concern for using real-time demand information is that companies will run out of supplies if they do not correctly anticipate demand. Well, we are not talking about zero inventory and are primarily focused on short-term shipment. Companies would continue to have their medium- to long-term plans. Inventory would be maintained at the warehouses. The only change is that shipment would be made when the product is sold or consumed, so inventory would not end up in the wrong places. Similarly, plants would produce only when a product is sold, meaning incorrect products would not clog the supply chain.

SIMPLIFYING NEW PRODUCT INTRODUCTION

Introducing new products is tricky. It is estimated that more than 70% of product launches fail within the first year. Companies spend millions of dollars on advertising and promotion to launch new products, so the cost of a failure can be high. A *Harvard Business Review* article[20] by Joan Schneider and Julie Hall found five factors that explain failed launches: (1) The product falls short of claims, (2) it isn't very different from existing products, (3) it requires substantial consumer education, (4) it has no market, or (5) its fast growth is unsupported by the company.

I will focus on the latter: Why can't some companies support fast growth of a new product? It is usually because of a mismatch between production capacity and market demand. Take, for example, iPhone launches. Apple always seems to struggle to respond to new iPhone demand. However, in reality, they have cleverly merged the supply chain with marketing. How? They introduce a new iPhone at a big event, with Cook striding across a stage. That builds buzz. They say it will be available by such and such a date. But, in fact, they intentionally keep the numbers available at their retail stores very low, much lower than actual demand. Huge lines form outside Apple stores, which is often covered as a news story—more marketing.

What happens next is that customers go online to the Apple website, order their customized iPhone, and pay. Apple sends the order directly to its subcontractor in China, Foxconn, which builds the phone to the customer's unique specifications. Then Foxconn ships the phone directly from China to the consumer in the United States.

Apple does nothing but come up with the design and then collect the orders and money. However, there is a risk to this approach for companies not as powerful as Apple. It may eventually turn off customers because of the long wait. Samsung and other phone manufacturers take advantage of this lack of supply to sell their products to consumers. Moreover, there is always the risk of order cancellation. It is a fine balance that Apple seems to have mastered.

The mismatch in supply and demand could also happen at the suppliers' end. The repeated delays that plagued Boeing's introduction of the 787 aircraft were blamed on an unexpected shortage of fasteners.[21] These are the nuts and bolts that hold the plane together. Aircraft production requires millions of them each year. With 567 orders from 44 customers, the 787 was the fastest-selling aircraft ever developed by Boeing or its European rival, Airbus. How could nuts and bolts hold up the launch of the most hotly anticipated aircraft in history?

The nuts and bolts industry was running at a high level of capacity. Due to design changes at Boeing, the suppliers were unable to meet the increased demand. The second problem was how long it took to ramp up production capacity. It was suggested that the fastener industry would not have sufficient capacity for several years because they had to invest in tools and equipment with a long lead time. Despite several efforts by Boeing, the problem took many years to resolve.

There are three ways to handle the mismatch problem. First, by making capacity flexible so that the factory can be quickly retooled to support new or increased demand. Second, by sharing demand information internally and with suppliers, companies can plan capacities. Demand information for new products has to be computed from the results of market tests, focus group inputs, and other sources of information. Making it available to everyone involved in the supply chain, including suppliers, can highlight potential issues early. Third, it may make sense to increase stocks of critical inventory to meet the surge in demand during launch and also to have excess capacity available in factories to meet any unforeseen increase in demand. Once the product is launched, and demand information is collected, the new product can then be integrated into the regular process.

SIMPLIFYING INTERNAL ORGANIZATION ALIGNMENT

Many organizations suffer from the "too many cooks in the kitchen" problem. Everyone has an opinion, but no one is willing to do the work or be held accountable for the outcome. The supply chain spans across multiple organization silos: manufacturing, sourcing, distribution, and others. So it is important to appoint a supply chain leader who is accountable for supply chain performance across these many organizational silos. A clear chain of command ensures that any problem gets fixed quickly. This may sound elementary, but command and control structures are not that common in business anymore. Most companies have moved to matrix organizations with multiple reporting lines, and chain of command gets confusing. Matrix organizations do not work very well in operational areas, as they obscure who is the ultimate decision maker.

The leader needs to communicate goals clearly to the rest of the organization to make sure that everyone is working off of the same sheet of music. He or she also needs to require everyone to report clearly on how they have met those objectives. I have used a cascading set of metrics and their targets to link supply chain metrics with other organizational metrics.

After metrics are aligned with the team, performance needs to be tracked on a periodic basis. A dashboard is created to highlight the areas where performance is falling short of the target. A note of caution: I have found that at times some individuals may fudge numbers by changing the method of calculation to avoid looking bad to their superiors. Thus, it is important to agree on a method of calculation at the outset so that reports will be accurate.

Once bottlenecks are identified, it is important to diagnose the root cause of the issues. Techniques such as fishbone diagrams are very helpful for this effort. The next task is to develop a plan to fix the underlying problems. For example, at a consumer goods client, the supply chain organization was having difficulty meeting its inventory targets for some slow-moving products. A root-cause analysis showed that production quantity or batch size was the problem. The company had invested in large equipment to optimize its manufacturing cost. This equipment produced the desired large quantities but was really only appropriate for fast-moving products, not for slow-moving products. Every production run created months' worth of inventory. The company decided to invest in smaller production equipment for its slower-moving products, which resolved the problem.

As problems are solved, targets can be reassessed to identify ways to improve supply chain performance even further.

SIMPLIFYING ENGAGEMENT WITH SUPPLIERS

Many problems arise from the interactions between internal organizations and different logistics providers and suppliers. They inhibit a supplier's ability to perform. While companies hire suppliers for their expertise, many internal organizations expect their own procedures to be followed by suppliers. But that is like mixing oil and water.

For example, at a high-tech company, the planning organization did not allow suppliers to interact with each other and controlled all communications. They thought that though the work was performed by suppliers, the high-tech firm would remain accountable for the business results. This created confusion with the suppliers since they could not anticipate when they would receive materials and whether they could respond to an order. Wasted hours were spent in coordination meetings. The simple fix was for the suppliers to coordinate with each other and flag problems for the company's planning organization to fix. This immediately reduced the noise, and coordination became smoother.

In addition to fixing communication issues, it makes sense to work with the leading suppliers, but not all suppliers, to help them fix their planning process. Instead of giving orders to suppliers, you can ask suppliers to manage the material inventory levels in the factory and deliver only when the plant consumes items. Suppliers should be able to arrange their plans based on inventory levels and production plans at the plant. By making this change to accountability, companies can ensure that suppliers manage the firm's inventory in a more efficient fashion.

FIXING SUPPLY CHAIN BOTTLENECKS

Clearly, the resistance to change by a company's leadership remains one of the main reasons for the poor state of supply chains in many businesses. But there is nothing to be afraid of, as change can be easily managed.

The solution starts with designing a new organizational model. I have used a simple model to help my clients identify the root causes of bottlenecks and then develop approaches to fix them.

The process begins with an organizational assessment that compares business results with business needs. This leads to an understanding of culture and norms that are valued in the organization. For example, it may show that troubleshooting skills in the supply chain team are valued more than fixing the underlying problems.

Once problems are identified, the root-cause analysis shows why the organization has accepted these norms. Typically, it points to problems with incentives and sometimes to lack of skills or a confused decision-making process. For example, the analysis may show that the supply chain organization is incentivized to produce as much as possible instead of to produce what's selling. Once such root problems are identified, the design of a new organization is made possible. New design starts with defining the vision for the organization that fits the business needs.

Organizational elements such as the decision-making process, incentives, and skills are then fixed, and this is followed by setting priorities and rolling out the plan. The rollout should start with leadership training, so there is an understanding of how best to communicate the plan to employees.

Once the leadership is trained and aligned with the new approach, key people from different teams are trained under a program that might be dubbed "Train the Trainers." Training has shown to be effective if provided by peers or someone within the organization. It leads to faster rollout and quicker acceptance by the employees. Once the training is complete, business results can be monitored for any adjustment required.

A large program for changing an organization, such as debottlenecking the supply chain, can take several years to implement and will require constant support from the CEO. However, discrete steps can be taken to measure progress and capture benefits throughout the transition. The organization has to stay apprised of progress through constant communication.

Incentives and metrics are important to discuss, as they come up regularly as the root cause of problems in many supply chain organizations. In many companies, members of the supply chain organization are valued for their ability to put out fires. They are rewarded for their efforts in saving the day and not for fixing the problem. They like to be seen as heroes. Unless incentives are changed and organizations are rewarded for improving performance systematically, supply chain bottlenecks will continue.

Metrics should also be reviewed to see if they are driving the right business behavior. For example, a key supply chain metric used by many companies is production downtime. The assumption is that plant downtime is bad because assets aren't being utilized. As a result, the supply chain organization is incentivized to keep the plants running, even though they know that some of the items will end up in a nonmoving pile and have to be scrapped at a later date.

A better set of metrics focuses on the overall performance of the supply chain, such as customer satisfaction (measured by the percentage of items out of stock, for example), the number of days of inventory held, or the overall cost to deliver products, among other things. Fixing metrics and incentives will drive better behavior in the supply chain organization and lead to debottlenecking.

As for the consumer goods company cited at the beginning of this chapter—the U.S. company entering the Indian market through a newly acquired subsidiary—it was soon realized that supply chain improvements would not be sustainable unless incentives were fixed.

A dedicated team under the guidance of the Indian subsidiary's CEO spent considerable time fixing metrics and incentives of not only the supply chain organization but also sales and marketing. The Indian sales team's performance was measured based on sales to consumers, customer satisfaction (percentage of items out of stock), and inventory held at the distributors and retailers. The same metrics were then applied to the supply chain organization.

Alignment of the two teams' metrics completely changed the behavior of both organizations. Instead of pointing fingers at each other, the sales and supply chain teams focused on fixing problems collaboratively. Each organization displayed a greater appreciation of the challenges faced by the other, and each made changes to accommodate those challenges.

Supply chain teams provided better insight into inventory and supply challenges. Sales teams started to provide information about challenges at the wholesaler and retailer levels that could impact the supply chain. The two worked as a team, which led to an improved and more sustainable performance in the market.

A company's supply chain can either be a drag on its performance or can be transformed into a strategic advantage. Traditional business models that depend primarily on product differentiation and marketing seem to have outlived their useful life. Supply chain reform, on the other hand, can provide a competitive edge in this environment. Debottlenecking is a key first step to enhancing supply chain effectiveness and will more than pay for the investment required.

Another business risk comes from overhead. Companies tend to borrow and invest in fixed costs—costs that have to be paid even when business is not doing well. These costs can put companies in bankruptcy. Involving the sourcing organization can make the overhead investment efficient, which will allow the business to survive when it faces a rough patch. In the next chapter, we will discuss the role of store investment in retailer success and how sourcing can help to manage these costs.

5

INCREASE RETAIL SUCCESS BY MANAGING STORE INVESTMENT

STORE INVESTMENT AND RETAIL SUCCESS

You may recall that this book began with an anecdote about Zara and TJX—two retailers that know how to succeed in today's tough retail environment. Its supply chain organization helps Zara respond to fashion changes quickly, whereas TJX's sourcing organization helps it procure merchandise that guarantees customers a unique shopping experience.

Not all retailers, of course, can copy the business models of Zara and TJX. At most retailers, the sourcing organization's role is limited strictly to helping to buy merchandise. In this chapter, though, we will look at how much greater a contribution sourcing teams can make when retailers involve them in the management of store investments.

If you are in any doubt about retail's precarious state today, just check out the business pages of your local newspaper, which are filled with gloomy reports that traditional retailers such as Circuit City, Radio Shack, Macy's, and Sears are either filing for bankruptcy, closing stores, or doing both.

Online shopping, through websites such as Amazon, usually gets the blame both for the demise of brick-and-mortar stores and for the dramatic fall-off in foot traffic at shopping malls. Consumers who still set foot in stores tend more and more to use them for "showrooming"—meaning that consumers come in to look, as they would in a showroom, but not to buy. If they see something they like, they make a mental note or snap a picture, then later buy the item at home online—for a cheaper price and free delivery.

There was considerable gloom after publication of the data from the 2015 holiday season, when, for the first time, online sales actually outpaced retail sales. Many took this as a further omen of the imminent death of brick-and-mortar stores. But then how can the retail success of companies such as Zara, TJX, and Costco be explained? These retailers are thriving and continue to open stores, not close them. TJX, for example, plans to grow the number of its stores by 50% from 3,700 to 5,600.

We all know that stores fail or succeed, in large part, based on the uniqueness of their merchandise. But they also live or die based on how skillfully management handles the little-discussed discipline of store investment—buying real estate, buying or leasing buildings, and maintaining and upgrading those buildings.

The concept is similar to taking out a home mortgage. If you max your mortgage out, you run the risk of bankruptcy if your household income falls. However, if you are careful about your loan, you will be able to make your payments even during difficult times. Our focus, here, will be on how retailers can optimize store investments so that they can weather downturns in profitability caused by changes in competition, consumer fashion, or economic conditions.

RETAIL INDUSTRY EVOLUTION

Let's look at how the retail industry has evolved and why investment in stores has contributed to making some retail models obsolete over the last 100 years. In the old days, local mom-and-pop corner stores dominated retail. In cities, people walked to stores and limited their shopping to what they could carry back home. They shopped for daily necessities.

Sears Roebuck pioneered the sale of household goods through catalogs for rural shoppers. The catalog business started with watches and expanded into jewelry, sporting goods, musical instruments, saddles, firearms, buggies, bicycles, baby carriages, men's and children's clothing, and much more. When automobiles became common by the 1940s, people could go farther and carry more. At the same time, household refrigerators allowed shoppers to stock more perishable goods. General merchants and department stores became popular, and local stores started to lose out. The larger size of these stores reduced the investment cost per transaction, and local stores could not compete on price anymore.

Malls began appearing in the 1950s as the population boomed and people moved from the cities to the suburbs. Starting in the 1970s, the big-box merchant arrived on the scene. These stores drove a lot of smaller stores out of business.

In the mid-1990s, the first shopping portals began appearing on the Internet. E-commerce allowed companies like Amazon and eBay to compete without having to make an investment in a physical store. Whereas a brick-and-mortar retailer's per-transaction cost included store investment, an online retailer had only to pay a minimal amount for a warehouse, plus shipping to the customer. Retailers ignored the magnitude of store investment costs at their peril. In 1980, seven of the eight largest retailers in the United States either filed for bankruptcy protection, were acquired, or otherwise became irrelevant.

STORE INVESTMENT

At most retailers, store investments are decided by a team called store development. The team members typically have a background working in stores and managing store operations. Store development is another area where sourcing teams are usually not involved. Given their background in store operations, most store development team members do not have a good understanding of sourcing tools and techniques. They end up using old techniques to buy services without understanding the underlying economic drivers. Three bids and a buy, a tactical buying process, is most commonly used for purchasing. It results in significant overhead costs for everyone involved, including the retailer, general contractors, and traders, and doesn't provide good pricing or establish long-term relationships with suppliers.

Our team has helped sourcing teams at leading retailers deliver great results for their store development organization. Sourcing teams can identify cost drivers and engage with general contractors and construction workers in a more strategic and cost-effective way. Developing long-term relationships with suppliers allows sourcing teams to reduce costs, reduce construction time, and choose the timing of construction when costs are not at a premium. The sourcing teams can also work with design teams to select store material that is both appealing to consumers and cost-effective. All these steps can reduce store construction costs and make them competitive against e-commerce sites like Amazon.

For example, at a multibrand retailer, our team reduced store construction costs by 30% by bundling new stores in California, and then contracting construction out to a few general contractors. Bundling of construction projects allowed general contractors to spread work throughout the year and reduce downtime during typical lean construction months. In return, they provided an attractive price to the client.

Of course, sourcing teams also need to develop an in-depth understanding of store construction. Buying services means buying work time from general contractors and workmen. Sourcing teams are comfortable with buying materials but struggle with buying services. Cost drivers have to be understood to come to a win-win agreement with suppliers. Unlike material costs, services costs cannot be reduced by buying in bulk from one supplier. Increasing work time or utilization is important for services buying. By purchasing in bulk, a lower margin may be negotiated, but a carpenter cannot labor around the clock to provide a lower cost. Reducing wait and travel time is essential to reducing services costs. We will return to the question of how to reduce such costs later in this chapter.

When a retailer can reduce its investment in stores and real estate, the decline in overhead gives it time to respond effectively to changing consumer demand and other changes in the market. Let's consider the different approaches taken by Macy's and Costco and see how those differences are impacting each merchant's performance.

MACY'S CHALLENGES WITH STORE INVESTMENT

Rowland Hussey Macy established R.H. Macy & Co. in 1858 on Sixth Avenue in New York City. He adopted a red star as a symbol. By 1877, Macy's had become a sprawling department store occupying the ground space of 11 adjacent buildings. In 1922, the company went public. It began to open regional stores and to take over competing retailers.

By 2015, Macy's was the largest U.S. department store company by retail sales and was the 15th largest retailer in the United States in 2014 in terms of revenue. It operated two divisions, Macy's stores and Bloomingdale's stores. Macy's was known for its niche in popular culture—the annual Thanksgiving Day Parade in New York City—and the diversity of its merchandise.

Macy's was no stranger to acquisitions, store closings, and bankruptcy. An acquisition strategy can provide quick growth but can burden the acquirer with debt and long-term costs. In Macy's case, it resulted in a hodgepodge of different properties that were less than optimal and proved difficult to integrate with the base business.

Macy's was again in financial trouble in 2015. Same-store sales began to decline due to warm weather in the United States, a drop in Chinese tourist spending, and the popularity of online retailing. The company's operating margins and return on assets have been consistently declining year-over-year. Macy's announced several store closings, starting in January 2015. There was concern that Macy's store closings would have a broader impact on the survival of malls where Macy's was the anchor tenant. Additionally, the retailer announced a series of cost-savings initiatives to reduce overhead by $400 million and apply the savings to growth. It also announced a plan to open a new off-price store called Backstage.

With more than 800 stores, Macy's is sitting on some prime real estate. But because of its financial troubles and the agitations of an activist investor, Macy's has announced it will consider spinning off (and leasing back) some of its properties. Such a restructuring could help boost its stock price in the short term but also could have a negative impact on Macy's profitability and survival long term. Under a lease-back plan, Macy's risks losing its ability to close, expand, or remodel stores in response to market changes. The company will also have to make lease payments. Of course, if market conditions deteriorate too much, Macy's can always file for bankruptcy protection again.

It is entirely reasonable for retailers to close stores from time to time to reflect changing consumer demand and foot traffic. The concept is similar to pruning a tree: You have to remove outer branches to allow the tree to grow in the desired direction. In Macy's case, however, the consistent drop in margins and in return on assets indicates that something fundamental in the retailer's business model is not working. Macy's seems unable to reduce investment in assets (stores) in line with dropping operating profits. The retail store provides a venue for commerce but can be the cause of bankruptcies when store revenue and foot traffic declines. To compete effectively against online retailers such as Amazon, Macy's must make a careful analysis to ensure that its investment in stores remains financially viable. A strategy of growth through acquisition has left Macy's saddled with inflexible overhead costs and debt.

Let's now turn to Costco and the different strategy it uses to grow its business successfully.

COSTCO'S APPROACH

Jim Sinegal and Jeff Brotman opened Costco's first warehouse in Seattle, Washington, on September 15, 1983. By 2015, Costco had become the second largest retailer in the world after Walmart.

Costco keeps prices low by buying in huge quantity and never marking up any product more than 15%, less than the typical 25% markup at a supermarket or 50% at a department store. Costco makes up those margins by charging a $55 annual membership fee to its 64 million members. They never advertise, have no signs in the aisles, and don't bag what you purchase. Costco has one of the most generous return policies in the industry. Costco comes out on top in customer satisfaction surveys and is rated among the top two retailers in the country. It is no surprise, then, that 91% of Costco members renew their membership every year. The company also pays employees twice the average wage for a retail sales worker, which also may help explain customer satisfaction. In addition to high wages, the vast majority of Costco employees also receive company-sponsored health care insurance.

Less discussed is Costco's approach toward real estate.

The company is estimated to invest $80 to $100 million on each new store. On average, a new store's sales exceed that amount within the first year of its opening. Costco believes it always has the option of waiting for a good real estate deal and doesn't get into an expensive war of the kind that Walmart and Sam's Club often indulge in to open a store. It walked away from land that it decided cost too much at a site in Dallas, even though the property met its other criteria. The company simply felt no pressure to make a suboptimal buy. Since Costco opens only 30 stores a year worldwide, if it can't find the right property, it just moves to another city, state, or even country, where a better buy may be available. It is a fundamental part of Costco's business model to keep costs down.

In addition to being careful about its real estate investments, Costco practices "no frills" construction. Its stores' floors are concrete slabs— more durable and easier to maintain than linoleum or carpet. Huge ceiling skylights help save on lighting costs. Merchandise is stacked on the industrial pallets at the store, saving millions on handling.

The difference between Macy's and Costco's store investment is their approach toward growth. Macy's manages store investment at a portfolio level whereas Costco manages it at each store level. A portfolio strategy assumes the inherent risk of acquiring (or building) some nonperforming stores to achieve quicker growth. Depending on demand trends, a company like Macy's may have to keep changing its portfolio by buying or closing stores. In contrast, Costco's thoughtful approach to store investment reduces risk by growing at a moderate pace, a conservative approach that survives business headwinds.

EVALUATING STORE INVESTMENT

Companies spend an enormous amount of money on store openings. A warehouse store may cost as much as $80 million while a big-box store may cost $15 to $20 million, and a department store may cost $2 to $10 million. To decide how much to invest in the store, retailers consider the store's annual revenue potential versus the investment with a metric called the sales-to-investment ratio. This is not an accounting measure but more of a rule of thumb to determine the limit for investment. Typically, the sales-to-investment ratio ranges from 1.8 to 2.5, depending on the margin level. Lower-margin stores will have higher ratios whereas higher-margin outlets will have a lower ratio. Beyond this sweet spot on the sales-to-investment ratio, it becomes difficult for a store to remain financially viable.

A retail client asked our team to advise them on how to improve their sales investment ratio. Figure 5.1 shows that the ratio has been declining steadily because of dropping sales per store and increasing stores.

Why is this happening? The retailer was going through a hyper-growth stage and was building lots of stores to meet the demand. As the number of stores increased, the availability of ideal space for opening stores became limited, so the company spent more money to acquire expensive real estate both in terms of location and area (square footage). The revenue was declining because the new stores were cannibalizing sales from existing stores. Because the new stores were not ideally located, they were not getting as much foot traffic as

Figure 5.1—Sales Investment Ratio Trend

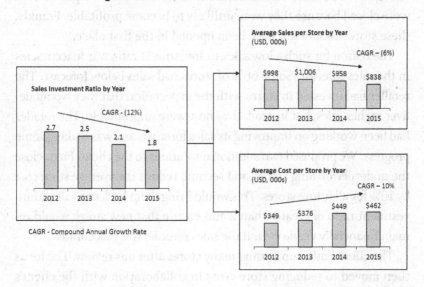

CAGR - Compound Annual Growth Rate

the old stores. Instead of waiting for the right opportunity to make an investment, the retailer was in a hurry to open stores to meet investor and analyst expectations.

Further analysis showed that the client had already opened many stores with a significantly low sales-to-investment ratio. These stores had no hope of ever turning a profit. For example, Figure 5.2 mapped the sales and investment costs of the retailer's stores in the Dallas metro area. Stores on the upper-left side, or the shaded area of the chart, had a sales investment ratio greater than 2. These were the profitable stores. The stores on the bottom-right side, or the white portion of the chart, had a sales investment ratio lower than 2. These were the unprofitable stores that needed attention. In the Dallas market, close to one-third of the stores were unprofitable. The stores that were near the shaded area were modified to make them profitable. The equipment and furnishing were changed to reduce investment or increase sales of these stores. Reducing investment in an existing store had limitations, as most of the cost was already sunk but the company planned to delay remodeling or spend less on remodeling. Also, investment in some expensive new equipment was delayed. The retailer could salvage 10% of these stores. Stores that were in the far-right bottom were closed because they were unlikely to become profitable. Frankly, these stores should not have been opened in the first place.

The reason for such a low sales-to-investment ratio was inaccuracies in the sales forecast. Some 66% of stores had sales below forecast. The retailer had invested in stores with the expectation that they would deliver higher sales, but instead, they now were unprofitable. The retailer had been working on improving its sales forecasts and was making some progress. We proposed two additional solutions to the client. First, close the underperforming stores, and second, reduce the average store cost by 10% for all future stores. This would bring them back to a sales-to-investment ratio of greater than 2 and ensure that new stores would remain financially viable even if the sales forecast was inaccurate.

The client ended up closing many stores after our review. The focus then moved to reducing store costs in collaboration with the client's sourcing organization, so all of the new stores would remain financially viable. The client found that the store development team was using tactical purchasing techniques and that involving the sourcing organization would allow them to form strategic relationships with

Figure 5.2—Sales vs. Investment Matrix for Dallas Metro Area

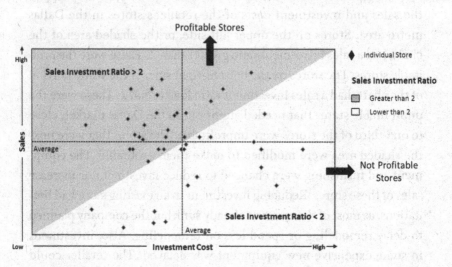

general contractors and other vendors. The sourcing organization would help the client understand underlying economic drivers for store construction and create strategies to reduce costs.

REDUCING STORE COSTS

Store costs are driven by three elements—real estate, construction, and the speed and timing of construction.

Real Estate Cost

The cost to buy or lease a store varies quite a bit from one location to another and from one city to another. In the case of our retailer, the cost was not completely under its control. Our team developed guidance on how much should be invested in real estate based on trends in regional sales. For example, the retailer made more money from stores on the East Coast than in the South. It was understandable for the real estate organization to acquire expensive corner locations in Manhattan. However, we suggested carefully investing in Dallas. We also agreed with the real estate group that the tenant improvement allowance (TIA) should be negotiated as part of the lease deal with the landlords. The TIA is the amount a landlord is willing to spend for the tenant to retrofit or renovate office or retail space. It reduces the fixed cost in opening a store. The retailer had a great brand and attracted high-end customers. Once it opened stores in an area, other high-end retailers typically followed, because they benefited from the foot traffic of affluent customers. This provided an excellent opportunity to negotiate a favorable TIA with the landlords.

Construction Cost

The construction cost was completely under the retailer's control. However, we found it varied quite a bit from one store to another, even though stores were all within a two-mile radius and had similar footprints and locations. The variation was due to tactical engagement of general contractors, construction workers, and material suppliers by the retailer. Our analysis showed that the company spent 68% of their store cost on general contractors and trades and 42% on store materials. Despite spending a large amount on store materials, the retailer didn't focus on optimizing the spending in this area.

General Contractors and Builders

General contractors (GC) are responsible for the day-to-day over-sight of a construction site, management of vendors and construction workers, and the communication of information to all involved parties throughout the course of a building project. They specialize in construction and coordinate with client teams to ensure projects are completed to the agreed quality, time, and budget. Depending on the nature of the project, they provide all of the material, labor, and equipment. They hire specialized subcontractors or workers to perform all or portions of the construction work. Their responsibilities may include engineering, applying for building permits, providing temporary utilities on-site, managing personnel on-site, monitoring schedules and cash flow, maintaining accurate records, and disposing of or recycling construction wastes.

A construction worker is a manual worker who specializes in a craft requiring particular skills. These specializations may include roofing, plumbing, and electrical wiring. Some construction trades may require licensing and several hours of recertification every year. The workers might work independently or supervise a crew on the project, depending on its size and the complexity of the work.

Returning to our client example, the client team contracted with the general contractor and construction crews on an ad hoc three-bids-and-a-buy process. It was a tactical contracting process where the retailer received bids from three general contractors for each site and chose the best one. Due to a large amount of building, the process created a lot of work for the general contractors because they had to bid for each site separately. It also created extra work for the client's staff because they had to review proposals for each location. It increased the overhead cost for everyone.

The three-bids-and-a-buy process did not leverage the general contractors' market knowledge or develop long-term relationships with them. Due to this tactical engagement, the general contractors did not provide favorable rates, and some chose not to bid. In most cases, the client did not receive three bids and ended up working with a single general contractor for most sites. The projects were negotiated based on historical rates—not capturing the benefits of a changing supply market.

The cost of any change after the bids were accepted fell on the retailer. Our analysis showed that the retailer paid an additional 25% on change fees for alterations made to the construction drawings after bidding. We suggested two approaches to the retailer's sourcing organization to help them reduce the cost of general contractors and construction workers.

First—Group Projects and Sequence Them Throughout the Year

Grouping the projects in a geographical location and spreading them throughout the year allowed the general contractors to spread overhead across multiple projects and to balance workload on construction workers throughout the year. Also, we suggested that the retailer consider using remodeling projects to balance the workload for general contractors between new store construction projects. The bundling of projects reduced cost because it reduced the general contractors' costs for bidding for different projects. This, in turn, delivered reduced change order costs because the general contractors became responsible for ensuring the drawings reflected the ground conditions. It also lowered the cost for construction workers who spent more time working and less time waiting between jobs.

Figure 5.3 shows the construction of projects across the United States. As you can see, there were a large number of building projects

Figure 5.3—Construction Projects: By City

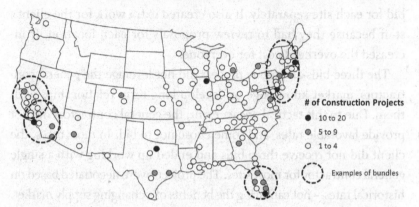

# of Construction Projects
- ● 10 to 20
- ◐ 5 to 9
- ○ 1 to 4

⟨ ⟩ Examples of bundles

planned in the New York area, South Florida, and Northern and Southern California. Many of these projects fell within an easy driving radius. These stores were grouped or bundled. Of the 1,100 stores that were planned for construction or remodeling, 70% were successfully bundled for construction purposes.

Second—Move Toward Strategic Relationships with General Contractors

The three-bids-and-a-buy process was discarded, and a more strategic approach was introduced. The bundling of projects allowed for early engagement with general contractors. They became more involved in the design phase and provided feedback on different assumptions. The new process also allowed for the robust selection of general contractors. They were selected based on their capability to meet future requirements and performance. Also, they were chosen for their overall value, including quality standards, schedule compression, and lower costs. Figure 5.4 is the schematic of the old versus the new process. The new process encouraged feedback to the general contractors and the setting up of a process for tracking performance. The performance data were then used for selecting general contractors in future years.

Figure 5.4 — Bundle Bids vs. Three-Bids-and-a-Buy Process

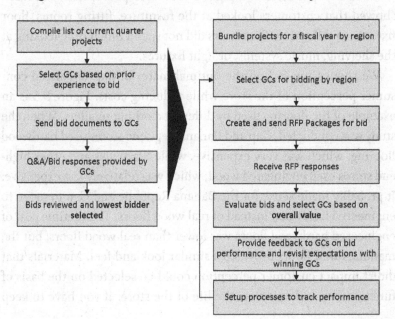

Store Materials

Store materials consist of building materials, furniture, equipment, and IT. The design and sourcing organization divided these materials into two categories—materials that impact customers' perception while they shop in the store and materials that are not visible to customers. It made sense to spend more on materials that influence customer perception and less on other materials. The materials that impacted customers' perception of a store, however, varied from one brand to another. For example, if you consider Banana Republic and Old Navy, stores owned by the same retailer but targeted at different customer segments, higher-end customers at Banana Republic are more attuned to store aesthetics than cost-sensitive consumers at Old Navy. Flooring may have a substantial impact on customer perception at Banana Republic stores but will not be that important for Old Navy stores.

There were constant arguments between different teams about which materials impact customer perception. The design team claimed every material impacted customer perception. Research showed that customers looked at the furniture, fitting rooms, floor fixtures, and flooring. Customers did not spend much time looking at the shelving, music systems, or light fixtures.

We spent time to find the optimal material that enhanced consumer perception of the store while reducing costs. Figure 5.5 is an example of the flooring used by different clothing retailers. When the study was conducted, Gap and Banana Republic stores used hardwood flooring, which was very expensive, while Starbucks and other high-end stores used engineered wood, which was relatively less expensive. It probably made sense for the Banana Republic and Gap to move to engineered hardwood instead of real wood floors. The lifetime cost of engineered hardwood floors was lower than real wood floors, but the manufactured floors provided a similar look and feel. Materials that didn't impact customer perception could be selected on the basis of functionality and cost over the life of the store. If you have to keep

Figure 5.5—Flooring: Cost Improvements by Standardization

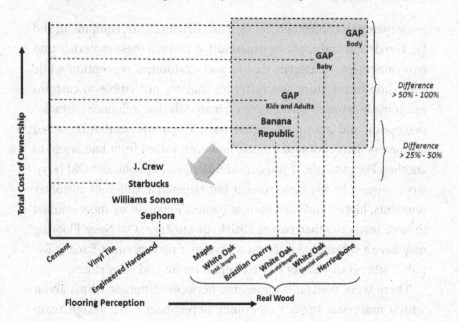

replacing bulbs every few weeks, saving money with cheaper bulbs is less important than the inconvenience it would create for day-to-day operations of the store.

Once the store materials were finalized, suppliers were selected for the value they provided to the retailer. We found that it was best to put store materials out to bid every two to three years because suppliers introduce new products in that time frame. At a financial services client, we found that seeking bids for furniture could potentially reduce the cost by 30%. Furniture suppliers introduce new designs all the time, and there was merit in evaluating the standards at a regular interval.

In addition to finalizing the design, we found that centralizing store material purchases significantly reduced cost. To avoid potential construction delays, the retailer historically bought materials at the construction site and did not buy them centrally. Combining volume across all stores provided significant discounts and also improved services. Suppliers were willing to ship materials directly to the site if a schedule was provided in advance. About 80% of the store material procurement was centralized and purchased through corporate contracts. The remaining 20% involved smaller purchases, and they continued to be made locally during construction.

Speed and Timing of Construction

Store construction took anywhere from three to six months, depending on the location and size of the store. A store does not generate revenue while it is being built; thus, reducing construction time increases revenue. Construction costs depend to a large extent on the time required to build. For example, labor costs are determined by the number of days for construction.

The construction methods used by the retailer also had not changed in a long time and were not optimal. If you have been to any construction site, you know that construction crews are not utilized 100% of the time. They wait for materials to be delivered and for other crews to finish their jobs. The problem is worse at construction sites where there is no place to store material. This is particularly true if you are building in a working mall.

Our client's project managers and general contractors made every effort to reduce the waiting time by planning ahead. But there was still a lot of downtime on the construction site.

The retailer had been experimenting with ways to speed up construction. We proposed the idea of first building the store in an empty warehouse, fitting all the pieces together like a jigsaw puzzle, and then disassembling the pieces and packing them in a container. The packing was done in a way so that construction crews would unload the first day's material first, the second day's material second, the third day's third, and so on, following the sequence of the construction. This reduced waiting time for material and eliminated delays for such common problems as the delivery of wrong material. This approach reduced the construction time by half. The sourcing organization negotiated the details of the deal with different providers to make it happen.

The timing of construction also has an impact on cost. If you have remodeled your house, you probably know that construction crews are busiest during summer. Everyone wants to remodel during the spring and summer, and you end up paying a premium. Similarly, store construction crews are busy during the third quarter. Every retailer wants to build or remodel their stores in the third quarter so they will be ready in time for Christmas shopping.

At the client, we found that general contractors and construction crews charged a premium as high as 100% to work during the third quarter. The best time to build from a cost perspective is in the fourth quarter when no one is building. Planning ahead and sequencing construction projects significantly reduced the construction premium. Bundling projects provided an uninterrupted workload to the general contractors and construction crews, which contributed to better pricing during the third quarter as well.

SIMPLIFYING STORE DEVELOPMENT

The store development process at many retailers gets bogged down. As retailers struggle with sales, they tend to change the store designs to make them more relevant to changing consumer tastes. But the result is often a confusing store design from the consumer perspective as well as add significant complexity in the construction process. We suggest a three-step procedure to simplify the store development process by involving the sourcing organization.

STEP 1—FOCUS INTERNAL RESOURCES ON STRATEGIC AREAS

Many retailers do too much of their construction in-house. Some still do their own architectural drawings, and some still have in-house project managers—this despite the fact that today there are good architectural and project management firms that can provide quality work. Outsourcing some functions allows retailers to focus more on strategic areas and allows a third party to manage day-to-day tasks. A third party can also bring the latest innovations while lowering costs. There is a range of options available to retailers, depending on their appetite for outsourcing. The sourcing organization can help in identifying the best solutions and the right suppliers for each of these areas.

- For smaller retailers like Tiffany's with a few hundred stores, it probably makes sense to do most of the store development work in-house. Though they would benefit from outsourcing by leveraging scale with other retailers, they do not have sufficient volume to get attention from outsource providers. Construction and facility management services could be partially outsourced. In-house management provides more flexibility regarding design and execution. On the flip side, however, doing everything in-house can burden real estate leadership with day-to-day issues and distract it from longer-term goals.

- For midsized retailers, such as Ann Taylor or Nike with 1,000 stores, it makes sense to outsource everyday activities such as construction and facility management services. They should also consider partially outsourcing property and project management services. Outsourcing activities of lower strategic value frees up the real estate team to focus on longer-term objectives.

- For larger retailers like Starbucks and McDonald's with thousands of stores worldwide, it probably makes sense to keep strategy in-house but to outsource other services as far as possible. They have a large enough scale for outsourcing and can get excellent deals from suppliers.

Figure 5.6 explains the sequence for outsourcing, from performing almost all activities in-house to outsourcing everything except strategic areas. What's right for a retailer depends on their corporate philosophy. Since supply markets have matured, most retailers will surely benefit from some outsourcing and having their in-house teams focus on strategic areas.

Figure 5.6 — Store Development Outsourcing Continuum

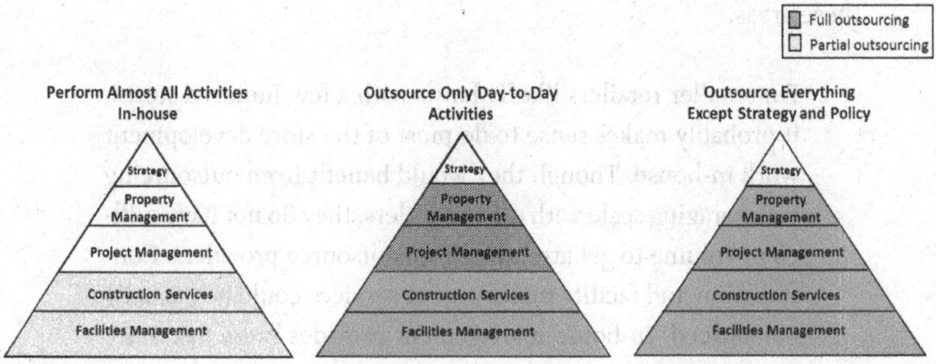

STEP 2—REDUCE COMPLEXITY

Store development organizations are responsible for ensuring that store designs are contemporary and fresh. The design has to be appealing so when consumers walk into the store, they feel comfortable spending time there. Once consumers are in the store, it is the merchandise or products that entice them to buy. Store development organizations need to update designs every two to five years to keep them relevant with changing consumer tastes. Like any design process, the extent of the redesign can create a lot of work. It can also result in scrapping store materials and furniture held in warehouses at a cost of millions of dollars.

A better approach is to change store designs gradually by focusing on a few critical elements of the store. The sourcing organization can help by researching trends in the market and finding the right suppliers for major design elements. Suppliers can smooth the change so that scrapping or holding nonmoving inventory is not required.

STEP 3—ALIGN INCENTIVES

The store development process touches many organizations at a retailer. It starts with the sales organization developing plans to open new stores or remodel existing ones. The process then moves to the store development team, which is responsible for creating the store template. The procurement team buys materials and services, while construction teams actually build the stores. The incentives provided to all these organizations are different. The sales development organization is incentivized to open a certain number of stores in a year, the design team is incentivized to maintain a brand image, and the procurement organization is incentivized to keep the cost down while the construction group is rewarded for building as many stores as possible.

Sometimes the incentives result in conflict. The sales organization tries to open the targeted number of stores whether the stores make money or not. The procurement organization is in constant conflict with the design team on cost. The construction group focuses on getting the stores built, irrespective of the cost and in constant battle with the procurement organization.

Adopting a standard set of incentives across the organization has shown to improve results and promote collaboration. Rules of thumb, such as only opening stores that meet a certain sales-to-investment ratio, can be broken down into organizational silos. For example, the sales team can be given a sales target in each region for all new or remodeled stores. Design, procurement, and construction teams can be given cost targets that they have to meet when constructing or remodeling stores. Once these incentives are fixed, collaboration across organizational silos becomes easier.

DRIVING RETAIL SUCCESS WITH SOURCING

The brick-and-mortar retail business model is not dead. Consumers still flock to different retail sites every day. What has changed over time is that some retailers have lost their focus on the economics that drive their business. They have become more focused on selling and less on managing the investment in their stores. Store development organizations have become an obstacle to the success of retailers in the changing marketplace. Their practices and approaches are out of date.

A sourcing organization can help change many of the practices used by store development organizations. It starts by collaborating with design teams to ensure that stores can deliver on the predicted sales-to-investment ratio. Furthermore, the methods for hiring general contractors and construction crews have to change. A more strategic bundling approach can improve general contractor and crew utilization and help in developing longer-term relationships. Reviewing the design of store materials and leveraging volumes nationally can reduce costs significantly. Additionally, the sourcing organization should work with construction teams to reduce the time taken to build stores. Many innovative approaches can be adopted without disrupting the construction schedule.

A thoughtful process for managing change can ensure better collaboration between different functional groups. Aligning incentives is the first step. Encouraging collaboration among the various teams will harness the best ideas across the organization. The CEO and organizational leadership have a vital role to play in this.

In the next two chapters, we will change gears and discuss how sourcing organizations can improve profitability from areas that are traditionally kept out of their purview. We will discuss marketing and outsourcing—two areas that are dramatically changing. They deal with services that do not conform to the traditional sourcing approach of competitive buying. They require a different set of skills and tool kits.

IMPROVE PROFITABILITY FROM AREAS THAT ARE CURRENTLY OUT OF SCOPE FOR SOURCING ORGANIZATIONS

IMPROVE PROFITABILITY FROM AREAS THAT ARE CURRENTLY OUT OF SCOPE FOR SOURCING ORGANIZATIONS

6

ENHANCE MARKETING EFFICIENCY

EVOLVING EXPECTATIONS FROM MARKETING

This chapter describes the benefits of expanding the traditional roles of a sourcing organization into marketing.

Marketing teams in most companies are untouchable. By that, I mean they are given free rein and do not need to reach out to other organizations. Sourcing teams are kept out of the loop and typically are asked only to cut purchase orders once marketers have negotiated deals with suppliers.

But marketing is changing in the digital age. Old techniques do not work anymore. Company leaders no longer want to invest money based merely on promises of revenue growth. They want to know what it will cost them to get that growth. Their focus now is on marketing's ROI.

I have helped sourcing teams deliver great results for marketing organizations. Sourcing teams can bring to the table analytical tools that help marketing campaigns become more efficient. They can help marketers negotiate better deals with suppliers. To do that, however, sourcing teams must develop an in-depth understanding of marketing.

Companies tend to partner with marketing suppliers for the long term. It is difficult to switch these entrenched (or "strategic") suppliers without significantly impacting the long-term branding of products.

Sourcing teams typically are not trained to negotiate with strategic suppliers. They do not understand the cost drivers that would allow marketers and suppliers to arrive at a win-win deal. Instead, they try to get better deals by pitting one supplier against another. But with marketing a collaborative approach, rather than a confrontational one, is what's required. This chapter explains how, by using such a win-win approach, cost can be reduced and ROI increased in several key marketing areas.

MARKETING BY COCA-COLA

Let's review how cost has become an important factor in marketing, using an example from Coca-Cola, the iconic American soft drinks company. John Pemberton, who served as a colonel in the Confederate Army during the Civil War, established Coca-Cola in 1886 in Atlanta, Georgia. Asa Griggs Candler, a businessman, bought the company two years later.

The success of Coca-Cola was mainly due to Candler's aggressive marketing of the product. After all, Coke is nothing more than sugar, carbonated water, and flavoring. Candler hired traveling salespersons to pass out coupons for a free Coke. He wanted people to try the drink, like it, and buy it later on. The concept is now popularly known as sampling, where a product or service is given for free to consumers to try before they buy. In addition to the coupons, Candler also decided to spread Coca-Cola's brand by putting logos on calendars, notebooks, and bookmarks to reach customers on a wide scale.

By the beginning of the 20th century, Coca-Cola had begun to spend a lot of money on marketing. In 1901, the company spent $100,000 on such promotions, and within 10 years the advertising budget had mushroomed to $1 million.

Coca-Cola flourished under the leadership of Robert Woodruff, who took over as president in 1923. During World War II, Woodruff pledged to make Coca-Cola available to soldiers fighting overseas for the price of only five cents. This policy greatly increased consumption of Coke. Even after the war ended, consumption continued to rise. In 2014, Coca-Cola had worldwide revenue of $46 billion and net income of $7 billion.

Coca-Cola spent a whopping $3.5 billion in 2014, or 6.9% of revenue, on advertising. In comparison, PepsiCo spent $2.3 billion, or 3.4% of revenue, and Dr. Pepper Snapple Group, Inc. paid $473 million, or 7.7% of revenue. Coca-Cola remains the number-one advertiser in the beverage industry. This massive advertising spending allowed Coca-Cola to gain a competitive advantage in major areas. It has helped successfully introduce new products into the marketplace, increased brand awareness and brand equity among consumers, increased the knowledge and education of consumers, and increased overall sales.

Despite Coke's marketing power, in the last several years concerns about sugary drinks contributing to America's obesity epidemic have had an impact on the company's revenue. In 2009, the company changed its marketing and media spending strategies from ads to in-store promotions and loyalty points programs. This move was a clear sign that Coke's advertising was no longer as effective as point-of-sale marketing. This dropped Coke's marketing spending from 9% of revenue in 2009 to 7% by 2011. To address the further decline in earnings, Coke has started a productivity program to save $3 billion by 2019 through a number of initiatives, including achieving increased discipline and efficiency in direct marketing investments.

It's not just Coke that's changing, either. Marketing is changing dramatically in the digital age. What helped Coke and others back in the 1950s does not work anymore. TV and cable companies used to be dominant media players and controlled consumer audiences. With the advent of online advertising by Google and Yahoo, marketing tools that were available to larger companies like Coke are now available to smaller companies. Companies are spending money with a variety of providers instead of just media companies. This includes digital media, data companies, service providers, and others. Marketing organizations often do not have the expertise or tools to manage these costs effectively, nor to negotiate with all the providers.

SOURCING ORGANIZATIONS' CHALLENGES WITH MARKETING

The sourcing organization can help marketing organizations develop analytic tools to drive the ROI and negotiate better deals with marketing vendors. Some of the work that used to be performed by outside providers, such as advertising and media agencies, can be brought in-house by expanding the role of the sourcing organization. In response, sourcing teams will have to update their skills and techniques. They must, for example, master the modeling skills needed to understand cost drivers and to identify ways to improve efficiency without having to rely on market competition alone. Sourcing organizations must also develop a deeper understanding of all the marketing services now available. By partnering, marketing and sourcing organizations can jointly increase ROI and create a plausible rationale for spending.

More and more companies are looking to make their marketing and advertising expenditures efficient, which provides an opportunity to expand the role of the sourcing organization. The focus is on spending money on "working expenses," such as media, and reducing money on "nonworking expenses," such as production costs and agencies. For example, you are making a video for your company. The money spent to create the video, such as payments for artists, production crew, and equipment, are all nonworking expenses, whereas money spent on getting that video to end user attention is a working expense. Both spending types are necessary; the question is where you want to spend more money. Companies like to spend more on working and not as much on nonworking areas.

LEVER BROTHERS' VS. PROCTER & GAMBLE'S APPROACH TO MARKETING EFFICIENCY

Many companies are adopting "zero-based budgeting" for marketing—a concept introduced by Kraft. Take, for example, the British-Dutch consumer goods giant Unilever, which was founded in 1930 by the merger of the Dutch producer Margarine Unie and the British soap maker Lever Brothers.

During the second half of the 20th century, Unilever diversified from being a manufacturer of products made of oils and fats and expanded worldwide. Its products now include food, beverages, cleaning agents, and personal care products. It was the world's third-largest consumer goods company as measured by 2012 revenue, after Procter & Gamble and Nestlé. Unilever was the second-biggest spender on advertising in the world, behind packaged products rival P&G, according to Adbrands.net, which compiles ad-spending data from several sources. Unilever is estimated to have spent $8.3 billion on advertising in 2014, AdAge reported.

In 2010, Unilever announced a reduction of its global marketer workforce by 12% and a reduction of its SKUs by at least 30% and said it was looking for other efficiencies in its ad budget. It reduced non-working media from 32% of total advertising and promotion spending expenses in 2010 to 24% in 2013. Most of its media-spending savings were from doing fewer but bigger marketing and promotional activities with higher quality and a greater impact on consumers.

Unilever, in 2016, announced a move toward zero-based budgeting for its marketing. This budgeting approach requires managers to start from scratch to justify marketing and other outlays. Despite this approach and other cost cutting, "Unilever's marketing spending will not necessarily decline in the absolute, or relative to sales," CEO Paul Polman said. To continue "outgrowing the market," he said, "we have to continue to invest in our brands." Unilever is looking to make their marketing spending more efficient in order to get more bang for their ad buck.

Procter & Gamble also sought to be more efficient with its marketing budget using traditional sourcing approaches. The company is estimated to have spent $15.3 billion on traditional media and online displays in 2014, a reduction of $2.64 billion, or 17%. The following year, P&G saved $370 million in agency-related costs. CFO Jon Moeller noted that the company had reduced the number of agencies it worked with by nearly 40% and cut both agency and production spending. It expected an additional $200 million of agency-related savings in 2016.

"These are non-working savings that will enable us to invest in advertising and trials of consumer-preferred products," Moeller told investors. "We are strengthening our working marketing programs—greater reach, higher frequency, and greater effectiveness at less overall marketing cost."

MEASURING MARKETING PERFORMANCE

The way marketing organizations used to justify spending is also changing. Historically, marketing teams based their spending for marketing and advertising on revenue growth. With branding becoming universal, and particularly after the 2008 recession in the United States, the revenue-growth argument was no longer accepted by CEOs and boards as a sufficient justification for marketing investments. Instead, there is now a focus on the concept of ROI, which was first popularized by Google, as a driver of marketing spending. ROI measures incremental revenue from a marketing campaign compared to what it cost the company to run the campaign.

ROI puts the focus on value, which is where the sourcing organization can help. Reducing cost alone does not make marketing more efficient. We have encouraged sourcing teams to work with marketing groups to develop an ROI measure. The objective is to identify campaigns that would provide better returns before negotiating with marketing providers and running the campaign. The math is similar to determining your 401(k) investment portfolio. For example, you might try to calculate if a particular fund in a 401(k) might produce a better return than another fund before making an investment decision. If you are not happy with past return and risk performance of a fund, you will move your money to another fund. The funds provide you with historical performance information as a guide for the future. For marketing campaigns, on the other hand, you have to find a way to test their effectiveness through test market or simulation.

Traditional methods of testing marketing effectiveness have severe limitations. In the past, marketing organizations test-marketed their new campaigns and compared the results with a controlled market. It took valuable time to test the campaign and also provided an opportunity for the competition to learn lessons from the test market. It assumed that consumers in the control market were not exposed to the new campaign, and therefore, the comparison truly reflected the effectiveness of the new campaign. But with the universal adoption of the Internet and online media, this isolation of a market became hard to achieve. Lastly, it assumed the cost of running the campaign in test markets was predictive of the cost for a nationwide launch. But media costs vary greatly by geography.

The sourcing organization can develop an analytic or simulation tool in collaboration with marketing teams to drive marketing efficiency. A computer model can be developed based on lessons from past marketing campaigns. The model can significantly reduce wasted effort while identifying ways to improve returns. It will simulate ROI by changing revenue and cost assumptions, and then optimize parameters to drive higher ROI. At a conceptual level, it looks something like Figure 6.1.

Let's take an example of a promotion plan for a product that works by giving out items such as pens, calendars, and diaries. Though promotion plans are relatively straightforward from a marketing perspective, a plan like this nonetheless will have multiple variables, such as the type of promotional material (pens, pencils, etc.), geographic

Figure 6.1—Marketing ROI

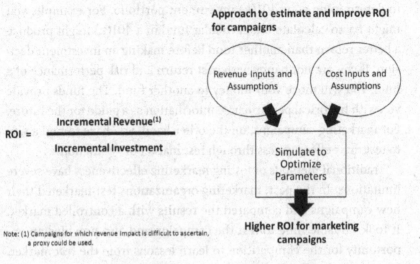

Approach to estimate and improve ROI for campaigns

$$ROI = \frac{\text{Incremental Revenue}^{(1)}}{\text{Incremental Investment}}$$

Revenue Inputs and Assumptions

Cost Inputs and Assumptions

Simulate to Optimize Parameters

Higher ROI for marketing campaigns

Note: (1) Campaigns for which revenue impact is difficult to ascertain, a proxy could be used.

coverage (distribution plan), volume (resource plan), and incentive for distributors to drive its impact. A computer model could be designed to test the impact of a range of options on ROI—for example, of different promotional materials, geographic locations (metros, regional, or national), volume (week, month, or quarter), and additional incentives for distributors (0%, 5%, 10%), along with costs. Such simulations can identify the right combination of variables to optimize ROI. The sourcing organization can then negotiate and finalize the plan with distributors and event coordinators.

MARKETING—COMPLEX SERVICES

In the 1990s, marketing and advertising teams primarily focused on television. TV got saturated quickly, and companies started to look at alternate ways to reach consumers. Advertising with Google, Yahoo, and other digital media became popular. There are now several tools available in the arsenal of smart marketing people such as community affairs strategies, public relations, and others.

Figure 6.2—Marketing and Advertising Spending Tree

Figure 6.2 is a spending tree that sourcing organizations use to map services that are part of marketing spending. The chart shows a range of complex services currently available to companies. Each of these areas or categories has several subcategories that a sourcing organization could effectively support. For example, the creative, production, and print category contains digital production, print and copying, creative services, and commercial printing. For a company with a large marketing budget, each one of these subcategories could represent millions of dollars of spending with suppliers.

The approaches needed to drive effectiveness in each of these categories vary quite a bit. I will review four services—creative agency, media, direct marketing, and market research—to show the benefits of using an analytical approach to improve efficiency.

CREATIVE AGENCIES

A creative agency provides services associated with creating, planning, and handling advertising (and sometimes other forms of promotion). Sometimes these agencies also handle overall marketing and branding strategies and sales promotions for their clients. Agencies believe that there is one golden rule for advertising: "It has to be creative." In other words, it has to break through the clutter. It is not just how ads are visually presented, filmed, or worded but how they pass on the message to consumers. Creativity works best when it makes consumers think about the product or brand.

Historically, the worldwide commission rate for agencies was fixed at 15% of the total billing. The 15% covered costs such as payroll and fixed and variable costs. Agencies tried to increase the commission, but most clients balked. From the company's perspective, paying agencies by commission did not provide the right incentive to make the advertising budget efficient. Under this approach, agencies had zero incentive to manage costs, since they benefited if costs went higher.

As with the previous example of P&G, many companies used traditional sourcing approaches to reduce the number of agencies and pressured them to reduce the commission rate. There were cases where some agencies were forced to lower their rates to 5% or 10% due to fierce competition from other agencies. But this could prove counterproductive, as agencies could then cut the quality of their output to ensure that they remained profitable.

So how does one determine how to pay creative agencies in a way that aligns with company objectives?

Many sourcing organizations have started working with agencies to develop cost transparency. The costs were broken down into direct costs, such as payroll and bonuses, and indirect costs, such as printing, shipping, and profit. They would audit the books to ensure the costs were paid and fairly represented in the contract. However, there was still no incentive for agencies to manage their costs effectively.

We encourage marketing and sourcing teams to collaborate to ensure they are achieving ROI targets. The labor costs are optimized through resource modeling, meaning that only the right resources are selected for the right campaign. For example, if a campaign requires creative resources to create a novel explainer video, then more money will be spent on these resources and less on resources that produce videos. Indirect costs are managed through a zero-based approach where agencies are required to justify the need for these indirect costs. Lastly, profits are made contingent on campaigns achieving their business results. Figure 6.3 shows how contracting with agencies has changed over time.

Figure 6.3—Ad Agency Relationship Management: Evolution

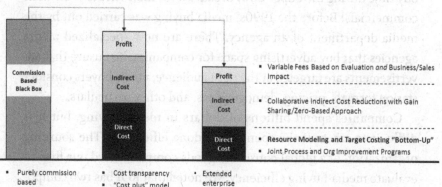

The resource estimate for direct cost is the most complicated, as it is difficult to figure out the resources required for different types of campaigns. Agencies typically use a rule of thumb to determine different types of resources needed to support an account, such as account management, strategic planning, creative, production, and research. These rules of thumb are frequently not accurate, and agencies typically run out of their creative resources. A better way is to model resource requirements on historical data, such as the number of creative teams per brief and other metrics. Depending on the number of briefs supported by the agency, the model can estimate resources needed for each type. It can then be used to project the agency hours and head counts required to support the company's marketing effort.

MEDIA BUYING

Media buyers negotiate and purchase time and advertising space on TV, radio, the Internet, and in print publications for placement of advertisements. You may have seen the famous commercials during football's annual Super Bowl. Media buyers in different companies buy time during the Super Bowl broadcast for their clients to air their commercials. Before the 1990s, media buying was carried out by the media department of an agency. There are now specialized media agencies that buy advertising space for companies. To ensure that advertisements are targeted at the right audience, media buyers consider station formats, pricing, demographics, and other particulars.

Companies spend billions of dollars in media buying, but it is difficult to assess if the spending is done efficiently. The sourcing organization of a global consumer goods company hired our firm to evaluate media-buying efficiency. We noted that ROI has two components: revenue and costs. There is usually a linkage between advertisement spending and an increase in revenue, but the exact impact is difficult to estimate due to many diverse factors. For example, an increase in ad spending by a competitor during the same time frame could potentially muddle the math. To avoid a debate on the exact impact of an advertisement on revenue, we developed a quality metric that can be used to optimize advertising spending. The quality

Figure 6.4—Ad Campaign Quality vs. Cost

Campaign Quality (vs. panel of like advertisers targeting similar audience in market)			Costs (vs. comparable advertisers)
Qualitative Element	**Core Campaign Elements**	**Weights**	**Should-Cost Methodology**
Reach / Coverage	The percentage of the target audience saw a campaign and number of spots bought to achieve it.	35%	1. Estimate costs of plan at standard rate
Targeting	The ability to reach the target audience.	25%	2. Adjust rate/cost for relative quality score based on cost benchmark
Day parts	The comparison between the percentage of Clients and percentage of competitors' ads in a part of the day selected for comparison.	10%	3. Adjust for scale
Center Breaks	The percentage of impressions that fall in the middle breaks of a show.	10%	4. Finalize Should-Cost and compare against Actual Pricing
Position in the Break	The percentage of impressions that fall in the 1st or 2nd position within a break.	10%	
Programming	The percentage of impressions in the top 20 rated programs. Top programs are based on the average target audience rating during the time period.	10%	

metric had six elements with weights that total 100%. Figure 6.4 shows how quality scores were computed for an advertising campaign for each brand.

For each element, a scoring method was developed on a scale of 100 and multiplied by weights to come to the overall campaign quality score.

In addition to the quality score, our team developed a should-cost model for media buying together with the sourcing organization. It started with the standard cost and then made tweaks needed to reach the right audience and quality score. Should-cost analysis determines what a product should cost based on materials, labor, overhead, and profit margin. To learn more about should-cost modeling, please visit http://ow.ly/AQvk3059OZR.

Note: GRP means gross rating point in advertising. It quantifies impressions as a percentage of the target population, and this percentage may be greater than 100 as advertisers try to make several impressions on their target audience to register the ad.

Figure 6.5 — Campaign Effectiveness Assessment

CAMPAIGN QUALITY	Weighted Average Score of Campaign Performance along Reach, Targeting, Programming, Dayparts, Centre Breaks, Position In Breaks (Worse 80 Better)	GRP's	Should Cost	Actual vs. Should-Cost		
				> +10%	+/- 10%	> - 10%
Brand 1	79	xxx	xxx	X		
Brand 2	79	xxx	xxx	X		
Brand 3	77	xxx	xxx		X	
Brand 4	81	xxx	xxx			X
Brand 5	84	xxx	xxx	X		
Brand 6	86	xxx	xxx			X
Brand 7	70	xxx	xxx	X		
Brand 8	72	xxx	xxx		X	

The quality scores and should-cost analysis were then used to assess the effectiveness of different media buying across brands. Campaigns that delivered higher than expected quality scores (more than 80) and had costs that were lower than should-cost were considered efficient. The company continued to spend on those campaigns. Campaigns that failed to reach their quality score or spent higher than their should-cost required tweaking. The placement of advertisements was evaluated to see if there were better times when TV spots could reach the target audience more effectively. The cost was optimized to ensure it was within the range of should-cost. Over several months, this optimization effort showed that the company was able to achieve better efficiency from their media buying with improved quality and cost performance. Figure 6.5 shows how campaign quality was measured, along with cost.

DIRECT MARKETING

Direct marketing allows companies to communicate directly with customers through a variety of media, including cell phones, text messaging, fliers, catalog distribution, promotional letters, newspaper and magazine advertisements, as well as outdoor advertising. Unlike advertising, direct marketing is attractive to many marketers because its results can be measured directly. For example, if a marketer sends out 100 solicitations by mail and 10 people respond to the promotion, the marketer can say that the campaign achieved a 10% response rate.

There are various channels available for direct marketing, such as email, online tools, mobile communication, and telemarketing. Direct mail is one of the oldest direct-marketing vehicles, and it is still popular. I still receive direct mail from auto companies, insurance firms, credit card companies, and museums. The cost of print and mailing makes this channel expensive, even though the U.S. Postal Service subsidizes it.

Our firm was hired by the sourcing organization of an IT outsourcing firm to improve the effectiveness of its direct-mailing campaigns. The company was struggling with a low response rate and increasing costs. We started the process by assessing the company's direct-marketing capabilities:

- **Customer Segmentation:** Were they focusing on the right segmentation based on past response rates?
- **Content Management and Creation:** Was the communication targeted well?
- **Data Management:** How were the lists purchased and processed?
- **Campaign Production and Execution:** How did the costs compare with similar campaigns run by other companies?

To improve the effectiveness of direct-mailing campaigns, our team suggested three steps to the client's sourcing and marketing teams:

1. **Customer Segmentation and List Management:** The should-cost model showed that incumbent suppliers were making high margins. The business was put out to bid to create competition and improve the quality of the mailing list.
2. **Printing:** The specifications for mailing were standardized across all direct-mailing campaigns. Work was consolidated among a few print companies, and better coordination was achieved among different groups within the outsourcing firm.
3. **Mail Distribution:** The post office provided cheaper rates for direct mailing if the zip +4 format was used. We developed plans so the company could maximize postage discounts by eliminating any mailing piece that didn't have zip +4 information.

Overall, this approach improved the response rate from 3% to 3.5%, while reducing the cost by 15%.

MARKET RESEARCH

Most companies hire market-research firms to identify and analyze the market need, market size, and competition. Market-research techniques encompass both qualitative methods, such as focus groups and in-depth interviews, as well as quantitative techniques, such as customer surveys and analysis of secondary data.[22] The market-research industry's worldwide revenue in 2013 was estimated at $30 billion. Nielsen, IMS Heath, IRI, and others lead the industry in the United States.

Most market-research projects are structured like consulting projects: A group of researchers reviews the primary and secondary data to identify underlying consumer trends. Typically, the research companies bring their own data as part of their work, but the data could also be bought separately. Over the last 10 years, much of the analytical work has moved offshore to countries such as India, while a small group of researchers works with the client teams on-site.

Our firm was hired by the sourcing organization of a leading biotech company to analyze its market research to improve efficiency. The cost of market research was increasing at a fast clip, and the company was concerned that money was not being spent wisely. The primary focus of the engagement was to understand where the money was used by market-research firms and, if necessary, to redirect the spending to drive better business outcomes.

As a first step, we looked at several past statements of work (SOWs). Our analysis showed that a significant portion of the money was devoted to professional fees for researchers who analyzed the data. A smaller portion was spent on surveys and in-the-field research expenses. Market-research firms also charged for travel expenses related to their researchers' visits to client offices. Figure 6.6 provides a cost breakdown.

Further analysis of the professional fees showed that much of the money was being spent on junior consultants who had just completed

Figure 6.6 — Market-Research Cost Breakdown

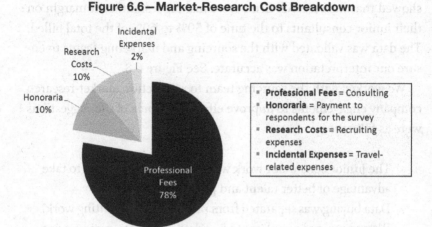

- **Professional Fees** = Consulting
- **Honoraria** = Payment to respondents for the survey
- **Research Costs** = Recruiting expenses
- **Incidental Expenses** = Travel-related expenses

Figure 6.7 — Professional Fees Breakdown

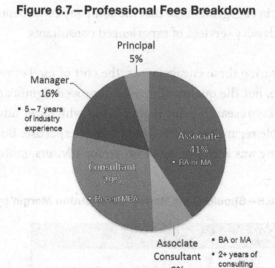

an MBA or had one or two years of experience. Only 20% of the professional fees were spent on more experienced consultants. See Figure 6.7.

Our team developed a should-cost model for the market-research engagements based on compensation information, which is publicly available, and compared them to the hourly billing rate. Our analysis showed that the research firms were making a significant margin on their junior consultants to the tune of 50% to 60% of the total billed. The data was validated with the sourcing and marketing teams to ensure our interpretation was accurate. See Figure 6.8.

We worked with the sourcing team to restructure market-research company engagements to improve efficiency. Some of the suggestions were as follows:

- The junior consultant work was sent offshore to India to take advantage of better talent and pricing.
- Data buying was separated from professional consulting work. We encouraged our client to buy data directly to avoid a price markup, and then provide it to the market-research firm.
- We recommended an increase in the time senior consultants spent in engagements so that the company could benefit from the advisory services of experienced consultants.

By restructuring these engagements, the cost of market research did not change, but the quality of results improved significantly. Previously, market-research firms would bring whichever advisers they had available regardless of the level of their expertise. But now that the company was spending more on senior advisers, more consider-

Figure 6.8—Should-Cost Model: Contribution Margin by Level

	Principal	Manager	Consultant	Associate Consultant	Associate
% of Billing	5%	16%	29%	9%	41%
Hourly billing rate	$450	$315	$265	$195	$150
Profile of Employee	• 9+ years of industry experience	• 5-7 years of industry experience	• MBA	• B.A. or M.A. • 2+ years of consulting	• B.A. or M.A.
Est. annual fully burdened cost	$340K–$400K	$260K–$310K	$180K–$220K	$110K–$140K	$90K–$110K
Est. hourly cost (with Utilization)	$405	$221	$136	$84	$62
Estimated contribution margin	10%	30%	49%	57%	59%

Fully Burdened Cost
- Includes:
  - Bonuses for employees ranging from 10% for Associates to 40% for Principals
  - Benefits such as healthcare costs
  - Taxes etc.

ation was given to selecting the right advisers for each engagement. Advisers were selected more carefully. The company benefited from the insights provided by the more-expensive senior consultants, while saving money by using cheaper junior talent offshore.

IMPLEMENTING MARKETING EFFICIENCY PROGRAM

Moving marketing organization focus from revenue growth to ROI is challenging. There are difficulties associated with incentives. Traditionally, marketing talents are incentivized to drive revenue growth irrespective of the cost. Incentives will have to be changed from revenue growth to ROI. Analytics become critical, and most creative people do not like analytics. They feel data and analytics will hamper their creativity. However, analytics will channel their creativity in areas that have the most impact on a company's revenue and bottom line. Driving the point requires constant coaching from senior leadership.

Also, it is difficult to recruit talent that has both creativity and financial acumen. Marketing teams do not usually have a good understanding of cost drivers. Involving the sourcing organization up front can help. Collaboration between creative marketing teams and financially focused sourcing teams can result in more effective programs at lower cost.

There is also a need for the sourcing team to update its skills and techniques. Modeling skills are crucial to understanding cost drivers and identifying ways to improve effectiveness. Many sourcing organizations have limited modeling capability and lack understanding of marketing. Instead, they depend on market competition to drive results. Traditional sourcing approaches may not work well. Sourcing organizations need better tool kits and talent to engage effectively with their marketing colleagues.

Ever since Coca-Cola began giving away those 19th-century coupons for a free drink, sourcing organizations and marketing teams have had to collaborate for the good of the company. In the current challenging ad environment, changing focus from counting eyeballs to achieving ROI can help companies justify investment in marketing campaigns. This collaboration between marketing and sourcing should drive better results.

Outsourcing is another area that is typically kept out of the purview of sourcing organizations. Functional leaders have outsourced portions of their organization with help from leading consulting firms. However, many of these relationships failed to deliver on the primary objective of cost reduction. Sourcing organizations can reduce cost by focusing on optimizing services in the local market. In the next chapter, we will review facilities and real estate industry outsourcing trends and how sourcing can help companies make smart choices.

7

SMART REAL ESTATE OUTSOURCING

NEED FOR SMART OUTSOURCING

Outsourcing has been trending in the business world for the last 20 years. It started with IT and then expanded to other areas such as payroll, finance, and real estate. Each of these areas is considered non-core for the business and, therefore, can be given to a third party to manage.

Until recently, sourcing organizations have had only limited involvement in structuring outsourcing deals or defining how to measure their success. This is primarily due to a perception from leadership that the sourcing organization lacks a deeper understanding of business and therefore can only play tactical negotiation or contract finalization roles in outsourcing deals. Here, we will focus on real estate and facilities outsourcing and how involving sourcing organizations can drive smart choices.

The facilities management organization provides day-to-day services, such as cleaning, security, catering, moving people from one office to another, and many others. See Figure 7.1. These are daily services but not core to most businesses. Nonetheless, it is an area of significant expense in a typical company's profit and loss account. We will discuss how sourcing organizations can help facilities teams to drive value for their companies.

The primary reasons for outsourcing, irrespective of the business area, are reducing costs; freeing up internal resources to focus on strategic objectives; gaining access to better talent; employing someone else to clean up the mess; and, of course, sharing risks like day-to-day execution, liability, etc. Many CEOs get pressured by Wall Street to

Figure 7.1 – Typical Services in Real Estate and Facilities Management

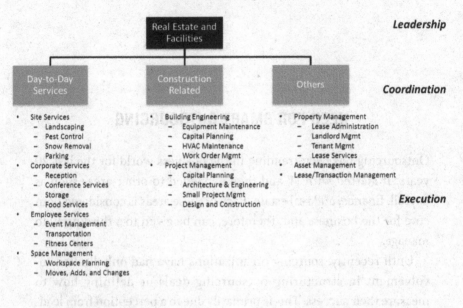

reduce head count during difficult times, and they use outsourcing as a way to get the necessary support for their business while minimizing internal staffing.

Outsourcing in real estate and facilities started in the 1990s with maintenance and cleaning services and slowly moved into other areas. Starting in the 2000s, the scope of work increased and the concept of integrated facilities management[23] (IFM) was born. It started to encompass diverse services, such as construction, project management, landscaping, janitorial, and food services. A large number of suppliers provided these services, such as CB Richard Ellis (CBRE), Jones Lang LaSalle (JLL), Cushman & Wakefield (C&W), Sodexo, Aramark, EMCOR, and many more. They primarily provided resources to perform outsourced work and also provided management oversight (i.e., acted as the middleman) to third parties involved in the area. Most of IFM provider cost was associated with labor. They charged clients for in-house resources and added additional fees for management services, oversight of suppliers, software and integration, and other services. See Figure 7.2.

Figure 7.2—Typical Facilities Outsourcing

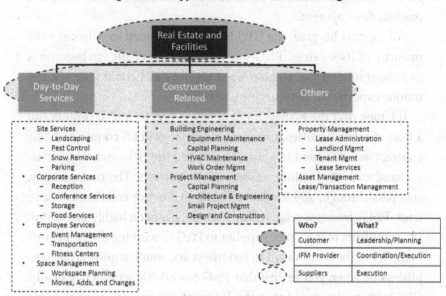

To understand how outsourcing in this space has evolved, let's look at Procter & Gamble. The company expanded globally in the 1990s and found its country-focused organizational structures a hindrance to growth.

FACILITIES OUTSOURCING AT PROCTER & GAMBLE

In 1999, P&G reorganized its small, mostly independent country businesses into global business units and regional marketing organizations. At the same time, it combined local support services into a single global unit called Global Business Services (GBS), which became one of the largest shared services organizations, consolidating more than 70 services, including facility management, real estate, accounting, and information technology.

A.G. Lafley, one of P&G's best loved and most strategic CEOs, took the helm in 2000 and focused on innovation. Under Lafley's direction,

P&G started to concentrate on its core competencies of marketing and product development.

To support his goal, the GBS leadership decided to outsource the majority of its services. P&G was ready for the challenge because it had consolidated and standardized services and could leverage the unique expertise of outsourcing partners.

JLL took over the management of offices and technical centers and a host of other facilities management services in 60 countries.[24] The contract was designed in a way that shared the risks and rewards associated with the facilities transformation efforts. The transparency, cost pass-through, and incentives facilitated better collaboration and trust. P&G's business relationship with JLL has been highly successful. JLL went from being a new supplier to P&G to winning the company's "supplier of the year" award in just five years, which is quite an accomplishment when you realize that P&G has 80,000 suppliers globally. GBS leaders also noted that the JLL contract had achieved the cost savings target.

COST SAVINGS VS. COST REDUCTION

Meeting a cost savings target, however, does not mean achieving cost reductions. These are two different things. Imagine total cost as your backyard full of weeds. Your contract with a gardener is limited to a small portion of the backyard, areas that everyone can see. The gardener claims victory if the weeds in that portion of the garden are reduced, even if the weeds in the other parts of the garden may actually be increasing and making your backyard look shabby. The way to fix this is to change your contract with the gardener, requiring him to weed the whole garden.

Similarly, the cost savings agreement in most outsourcing contracts focuses only on a small portion of the cost (a few services or a handful of projects), whereas cost reduction focuses on the overall cost (all services). Outsourcing providers claim victory when they meet cost savings targets, not when the overall cost goes down. Shareholders, CEOs, and CFOs, on the other hand, care about the overall cost or meeting a budget. The way to fix the problem is to increase the scope of cost savings to cover the overall cost.

Cost reduction, which is perceived to be the primary benefit from outsourcing, is often not realized. Our team recently interviewed 40 large companies across different industries that have outsourced facilities management. They found that 80% of the firms continue to emphasize the need for cost reduction. The focus is now moving from achieving a cost savings target to meeting budget numbers, which is the accurate measure of cost reduction. Facilities heads are being held accountable for meeting the budget target by CEOs and CFOs, and they are looking to make outsourcing providers more accountable. More and more deals are requiring outsourcing providers to write a check for the difference if they fail to meet the agreed-upon budget targets.

TRENDS

In addition to placing a greater focus on cost reduction, pioneers of outsourcing such as General Motors are actively looking at bringing some of the outsourced work back in-house to support their longer-term business strategy. Despite significant acquisitions, facilities outsourcing providers can perform only 30% to 40% of the work with their in-house resources. They generally must use third-party resources or other suppliers to perform the rest of the work, and they charge a fee (on top of their client fee) for managing these resources. New technology is making it unnecessary to employ an outsourcing provider, an intermediary between companies and their suppliers. With newer technology, companies can directly work with a large number of suppliers in real time, without having to pay expensive fees to the outsourcing providers or needing a large number of in-house resources to manage suppliers.

Companies can use their sourcing organizations to determine if outsourcing is the right strategy and how best to do it. Even if a company has outsourced a part of its business, it is always better to continually evaluate if it should change the structure of its contracts because the technology and business models of the outsourcing industry are evolving rapidly.

FACILITIES OUTSOURCING: TRANSITIONING TOWARD FULL SERVICE

In the 1990s, companies started looking at outside providers that would take over their facilities staff and provide services in a consistent fashion. These were not high-paying jobs, work could easily be standardized, and companies preferred to have other firms managing their problems. Outsourcing started with maintenance and cleaning services and slowly moved into other areas. The market was immature with many suppliers, and customer expectations were unsure. Understanding customer culture became important to deliver results, and account management became important for the providers.

Starting in the 2000s, the scope of work increased and the concept of IFM was born to meet the demand for such diverse services as project management, landscaping, construction, janitorial, food, energy management, and others.

Eventually, the deal size increased to hundreds of millions of dollars. The market consolidated with acquisitions and, similar to P&G's contract with JLL, cost-plus pricing became the norm. A cost-plus contract ensured IFM providers would earn a fixed margin as they passed on cost increases to their customers. As risk declined, IFM providers became a staff augmentation supplier—providing staff working under the guidance of the client team. The focus moved from providing value to providing added services. They were happy with lower margins and longer-term contracts that paid for their resources plus a fair

Figure 7.3—Revenue Streams for JLL

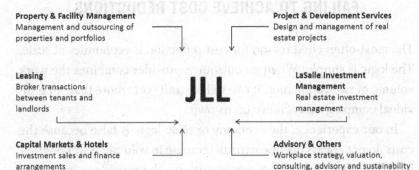

Property & Facility Management
Management and outsourcing of
properties and portfolios

Project & Development Services
Design and management of real
estate projects

Leasing
Broker transactions
between tenants and
landlords

JLL

**LaSalle Investment
Management**
Real estate investment
management

Capital Markets & Hotels
Investment sales and finance
arrangements

Advisory & Others
Workplace strategy, valuation,
consulting, advisory and sustainability

Source: JLL

margin. As the deal size continued to increase, IFM providers started to grow their services through acquisitions.

To demonstrate how diversification has helped these companies, see Figure 7.3. It shows how JLL earns its revenue from a variety of sources related to real estate and facility management. It also describes the different services provided by JLL as companies bundle these services in ever-larger outsourcing deals.

After 2008, the market changed as the United States entered a recession. Client companies became more cost sensitive, and pricing pressure increased on IFM providers. Leadership at the client firms began involving its finance and sourcing organizations in contract negotiations because many of the outsourcing deals were structured in a way that costs did not decrease when revenues dropped. Company leadership became concerned with making its outsourcing deals more efficient. The deal structure began to change from cost-plus to more fee-at-risk, where outsourcing providers were required to put some skin in the game.

FAILING TO ACHIEVE COST REDUCTIONS

The most-often cited reason for cost reduction is economies of scale. The logic is simple: When an outsource provider combines the work volume of two companies, it can reduce unit costs more than an individual company can achieve on its own.

In our experience, the economy of scale logic is false because the costs do not always decline with an increase in volume. Why does that happen? When volume increases initially, the provider can change technology to reduce costs, but as the size increases, the operations become unmanageable due to increased complexity, and the cost eventually starts to rise. This is one of the reasons why mergers between two large companies typically fail to deliver cost savings.

Also, most IFM provider costs are associated with labor and not equipment. The economy of scale logic does not work with labor. Just because an outsourcing provider acquires another client, the person doing maintenance is not going to work twice as many hours. To reduce costs, the unproductive and duplicate work has to be removed so that the maintenance person can complete the job in the same number of hours. It is all about utilization—an area we will discuss later in the book. Changing work processes and improving utilization takes time.

Let's illustrate why cost reductions are frequently not achieved by using a client example. The sourcing organization at a financial services firm hired our team to review its facilities outsourcing contract and identify future opportunities to reduce costs.

Our analysis showed that total costs went up by 5% after outsourcing, which came as a complete surprise to the client. As shown in Figure 7.4, before outsourcing the client used to spend 20% on in-house resources and 80% with third-party suppliers.

After outsourcing, the split changed. The company reduced its in-house resources and moved work to the outsourcing middleman. The company then started spending 10% on in-house resources, 15% with

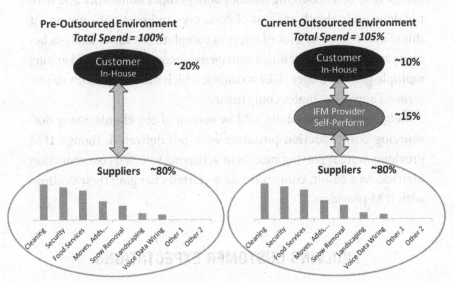

Figure 7.4—Cost Breakdown: Pre-Outsourced vs. Current Outsourced Environment

an IFM provider, and 80% with suppliers, thereby increasing the overall cost by 5%. This was despite the fact that the outsourcing provider claimed to have achieved all of its cost savings targets.

The increase in cost happened primarily due to the management fee charged by the IFM provider to manage suppliers and as its profit margin. The payment of a management fee was made with the understanding that the IFM provider would drive supplier costs down, which in turn would pay for the management fee, but this did not happen. Costs decreased in some areas but increased in others, and overall the supplier cost remained the same.

The IFM provider reported on projects that it was contractually required to track, but not on all cost areas. The key issue here was that of incentives. Similar to P&G's contract with JLL, the contract with the IFM provider was structured as cost-plus, passing through all supplier costs to the financial services firm. The provider had no incentive to reduce costs. The IFM provider was focused on the service side and hoping to provide additional service for increased cost.

Is this unique to this client? No. Most companies jumped on the bandwagon of outsourcing without doing proper homework and have not done an in-depth analysis of costs pre- and post-outsourcing. At this client, it took us a lot of effort to complete the above analysis because real estate and facilities management costs were divided among multiple general ledger (GL) accounts, which made it difficult to perform an apples-to-apples comparison.

Judging by the anecdotes told by several of our clients, many outsourcing cost-reduction promises were not delivered, though IFM providers were reporting success in achieving selected cost-reduction metrics. As a result, companies have started changing their dealings with IFM providers.

EVOLVING CUSTOMER EXPECTATIONS

Companies started changing their performance incentives for IFM providers. They started asking for performance against budget and also began to put the management fee at risk based on cost performance. There was an increasing trend for a guaranteed maximum price[25] (GMP) and fixed-price deals.

Some of these deals have a glide path on cost performance, that is, a declining cost curve. One leading financial services firm asked its IFM provider to reduce their facilities budget by 10% year-over-year. The contract specified that if the IFM provider failed to meet the target, it would have to write a check for the difference. This was a significant risk for an IFM provider because it has more than its profit at stake.

Other companies increasingly asked IFM providers to put the majority of their profit at risk, based on their cost performance. There were, of course, deals where IFM providers put only a small portion of their profit at risk linked to performance metrics (KPIs)—but the number of such deals steadily declined. See Figure 7.5.

Figure 7.5—Increasing Focus on Cost Reduction in IFM Contracts

Definitions

More than profit at risk - GMP and Fixed Price accounts where glide path and budget commitments require IFM providers to write a check if they fail to meet the cost targets

Majority of profit at risk - Accounts with fees at risk, gain sharing or performance upside based on cost performance

Small portion of profit at risk - Accounts that have fees at risk linked to KPIs primarily due to service

Risk

Spend ($M) by Contract Type

Increasing

15%

Increasing

45%

40%

Decreasing

SWINGING OF THE PENDULUM: DECLINE OF IFM

With the deals becoming more financially risky to the providers and smaller profit potential, the current model of outsourcing had to change. The pendulum is swinging toward reducing the scope of IFM by unbundling services and going back to having IFM providers focus on core expertise. Companies are starting to bring back supplier management in-house with the help of technology, and this reduces management fees.

Unbundling of Services

Initial rounds of outsourcing started with the concept of bundling services to get a better price from outsourcing providers, utilizing the economies of scale discussed earlier in this book. The deals got bigger and bigger. However, financial and bid analysis showed that the assumption—bundling drives better pricing—was found to be not true. Bundling reduced the number of outsourcing providers that could compete for the business. Also, many outsourcing providers ended up buying a number of services from other providers. This practice added the margin of the outsourcing provider on top of the margin of suppliers. Overall, the cost went up, and finance and sourcing organizations started to question the need for bundling.

Fees Under Scrutiny

There was a greater focus on the different fees paid to IFM providers and the providers' overall value to the company. Supplier management fees were under particular scrutiny. IFM providers routinely claimed that they were able to get better pricing from suppliers due to their size. What they failed to mention was the additional costs that were concealed in the price, which negated any savings, such as markup, additional labor, handyman services, etc.

Reducing Ability to Renegotiate After the Deal Signing

Another practice that came under review was the ability of IFM providers to renegotiate a contract after a fixed duration of service. IFM providers routinely bid low and then increased pricing after a year of service. More and more companies began to limit an IFM provider's ability to renegotiate the deals, either through contractual limits or just flat out refusing to renegotiate.

Pressure from Suppliers

As companies outsourced their real estate and facilities management, suppliers often found their relationship with IFM providers added little value to their performance. Many large suppliers preferred to directly work with customers. This was especially true for catering, security, and janitorial services.

Disintermediation[26] by Technology Companies

Technology solutions are being introduced that could disrupt the current model of IFM firms. These technologies are at the initial stages of development and could allow customers to manage suppliers directly without the need for IFM providers. The concept is similar to how Uber has challenged the traditional taxi industry by giving customers a very convenient alternative. Uber provided an app so customers could directly order a ride, removing the margin and overhead cost charged by the taxi company. Similarly, these technologies could enable outsourcing customers to manage suppliers without having to pay an expensive management fee to IFM providers.

DISRUPTING INDUSTRY— SHORT- AND LONG-TERM TRENDS

With IFM providers unable to provide cost reductions, real estate heads at companies are being asked to find alternate ways to deliver facilities services. They are being asked to collaborate with finance and sourcing organizations to develop these solutions. As we work with our clients, we see a short-term and longer-term trend.

Short-Term Trend—Unbundling of Services

More and more of our clients have started to discuss how to unbundle the outsourcing spending and bring some work back in-house to manage their costs more effectively. This means reducing the use of IFM providers to areas where they are strong.

One of the ideas is for the customers to manage large suppliers directly, to reduce costs and to have IFM providers manage smaller suppliers. The IFM provider management fee is linked to spending on suppliers. By managing large suppliers, the company may have to hire some internal resources, but the cost savings from management fees more than make up for the increased cost of new hires. See Figure 7.6, which compares costs.

The right side of the graphic shows how the future may look, compared with the outsourced environment that now exists, as shown on

Figure 7.6—Current vs. Near Future Outsourced Environment

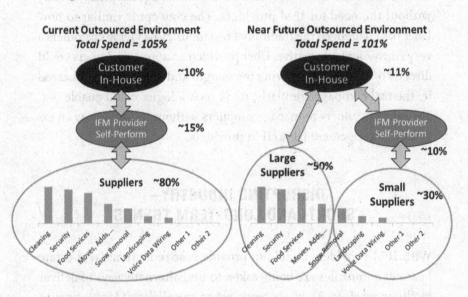

the left. In-house spending is likely to increase as companies bring aboard resources to manage large expense areas such as cleaning, janitorial, and food services. Spending on IFM providers will likely decrease because they will be only managing the smaller suppliers. Overall, costs are expected to decline through restructuring the arrangement.

Longer-Term Trend—Technology-Enabled Supplier Management

As with most other industries, the outsourcing industry is being impacted by technology. New technology is being developed that will make it easy for companies to manage their suppliers directly, without the need for an IFM provider. Figure 7.7 illustrates one such technology now in development.

With technology such as this, a company in New York can manage, virtually, suppliers working at their (customer's) site in Chicago. They do not need to depend on an IFM provider for coordination or over-

Figure 7.7—Example of Technology Platform to Enable Supplier Management

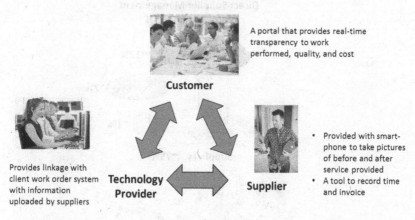

A portal that provides real-time transparency to work performed, quality, and cost

Customer

Provides linkage with client work order system with information uploaded by suppliers

Technology Provider

Supplier

• Provided with smartphone to take pictures of before and after service provided
• A tool to record time and invoice

sight. Most of the work can be automated and coordinated with the client team members at different sites. Also, these technologies are developed as stand-alone solutions, so the risk of hacking to customer servers is small.

Customers can manage suppliers directly with a small number of in-house resources, and they work with a technology provider to manage suppliers across different locations. The overall cost is likely to come down significantly, and companies will no longer have to pay an IFM provider to manage their suppliers. Also, transparency about supplier performance will allow companies to optimize their work patterns and reduce costs. We expect the overall cost will be significantly reduced by collaboration between sourcing and facilities organizations. For example, the sourcing organization can identify high-performing, low-cost local contractors for facilities organization and move away from high-cost national or regional suppliers. These local suppliers can be managed with the help of technology. See Figure 7.8.

Technology will also enable companies to reduce supplier cost. This is not about beating up the suppliers to get a reduction but about finding ways to remove non-value-added costs by understanding the underlying economies. For example, construction workers spend idle time at jobs because of unforeseen work stoppages such as un-

Figure 7.8—Future Outsourced Environment

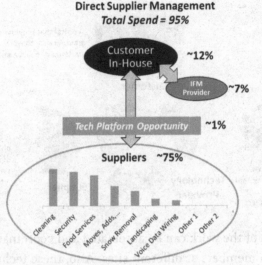

Direct Supplier Management
Total Spend = 95%

availability of materials. The idle time is a non-value-added cost that suppliers end up charging their customers. Technology can provide real-time transparency, which can help companies reduce idle time for construction workers by moving them to other jobs when there is an unforeseen work stoppage.

ENABLING COST REDUCTION WITH TECHNOLOGY

It starts with a focus on improving sourcing capabilities. Most of the spending in the facilities and real estate management areas is with service providers. As seen in Figure 7.9, 90% to 95% of expenditures are with services suppliers, whether we are talking about hard (construction-related) or soft (day-to-day) services.

The economic drivers for services spending are very different from material spending, as seen in Figure 7.10. Labor is the primary cost area for services, and it is determined by two factors—location and utilization. Demand and supply of a local market determine the wage

Figure 7.9—Spend by Supply Market/Category ($M)

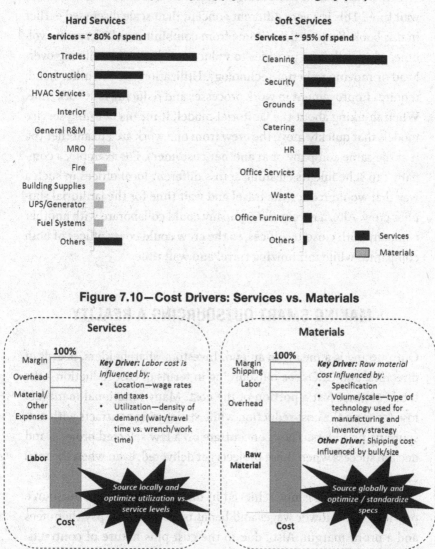

Figure 7.10—Cost Drivers: Services vs. Materials

rates. We all know the labor rate in New York City is much higher than the labor rate in other parts of the country. Utilization is important because a single maintenance person will not be able to work 24 hours nonstop if an outsourcing provider acquires more customers. See Figure 7.10.

Utilization means increasing work hours and reducing travel and wait time. This is a very different concept than scale discussed earlier in this book. Scale benefits come from combining and increasing volume, which allows a provider to reduce cost by better utilizing overhead or moving to better technology. Utilization, on the other hand, requires improvement in work processes and reducing nonwork time. When thinking about the janitorial model, it means defining service models that quickly move the crew from one work area to another (be it at the same company or at another customer). For example, a company can schedule its cleaning across different local offices in such a way that would reduce the travel and wait time for the janitorial supplier crew. Alternatively, the company could collaborate with another company with close-by offices, so the crew could cover offices of both companies while minimizing travel and wait time.

MAKING SMART OUTSOURCING A REALITY

Outsourcing is a means to an end. Investors, shareholders, boards of directors, and CEOs see outsourcing in terms of cost reduction—the total cost, not just a portion of the cost. Many functional managers lose focus on the cost reduction while structuring contracts with outsourcing providers. They concentrate on a few selected projects and declare success when those projects get delivered, even when the total cost increases.

Cost reduction is not achieved in many cases. Though outsource providers have lower wages and benefits, you have to pay them fees and a profit margin. Also, due to the cost-plus nature of contracts, outsource providers are far more willing to provide additional services for an extra cost. Both factors, fees and the cost-plus contract, result in an increase in cost, and not a reduction as expected when outsourcing these services.

So far, most sourcing organizations have had limited involvement in outsourcing deals. Many business leaders have directly worked with consulting firms to outsource a significant part of their business. With many outsourcing deals now under review, sourcing organizations can help companies outsource smartly. For some companies, it may make sense to bring some of the work back in-house, use technology to manage suppliers instead of using an outside provider for oversight, and drive value by collaborating with other companies where possible.

To reduce costs, companies should focus on suppliers or third-party providers. Most suppliers for facilities and real estate are local service providers. Sourcing organizations will have to develop the capabilities to source them effectively. Using standard competitive buying techniques, such as buying from China, will not optimize services costs. Improving utilization is the only way to reduce cost, but improving utilization is difficult. Sourcing organizations will have to work with vendors to develop service models that improve utilization in each of their local markets. For that, they would require transparency into supplier operations. New technology may help in providing transparency while simulation and other techniques are used.

In the next chapter, we will switch gears and talk about how companies can sustain changes. The concept of excellence is not just a utopia—it can be achieved with help from suppliers. Sourcing organizations have an important role to play in achieving excellence.

DRIVE BUSINESS EXCELLENCE WITH HELP FROM SOURCING

8

SOURCE EXCELLENCE

EXCELLENCE—UTOPIA OR REALITY?

For centuries, whenever humans have tackled any challenge judged supreme, their goal always has been the same: achieving excellence.

Both Eastern and Western cultures have been fascinated with the concept of excellence.

The sixth-century Chinese philosopher Confucius was quoted as having said: "The will to win, the desire to succeed, the urge to reach your full potential . . . these are the keys that will unlock the door to personal excellence."

Even Aristotle, the Greek philosopher who lived more than two millennia ago, took stock of excellence: "We are what we repeatedly do. Excellence, therefore, is not an act but a habit."

The concept of excellence soon found its way to business. I remember reading *In Search of Excellence* by Tom Peters and Robert Waterman when I was in school and becoming fascinated by the topic. Of course, what makes a company excellent and how it is achieved has changed over time. The desire to achieve excellence remains a key value in many leading companies.

Most business literature talks about achieving excellence through in-house resources. Today, however, with a significant amount of work being performed by suppliers, companies cannot achieve excellence without taking those suppliers into account.

In today's complex business environment, companies need excellent supplier partners more than ever. The definition of excellence should include working jointly with suppliers and third-party providers. When I talk about sourcing excellence, I am not talking about the excellence of the suppliers or sourcing organizations. I am talking about sourcing organizations and suppliers helping companies achieve excellence.

The mission statements of most sourcing organizations envision a partnership with business organizations. A key part of becoming a partner is to help business organizations achieve excellence. To do this, sourcing teams need to help business teams define what an excellent state would look like in two to five years, then help them to source it. The process involves developing an intimate understanding of the business along with knowledge of supply markets, which refers to a group of commodities or services including travel, hotels, and market research.

Let's look at how suppliers can help companies achieve excellence, using, as an example, the relationship between AT&T and Apple.

APPLE HELPING AT&T WIRELESS ACHIEVE EXCELLENCE

Cingular Wireless bought AT&T Wireless in 2004 to become the largest wireless company in the United States, moving ahead of Verizon Wireless and taking the AT&T name. Cingular CEO Stan Sigman told investors in 2006 that "our acquisition is working. At the end of 2004, we began a quest for industry leadership. We did exactly what we said we would. We can look back with pride. We had a great plan and great execution."[27]

However, Verizon continued to add more subscribers than Cingular, thus threatening the leadership position of Cingular. The mobile industry in the United States was changing, with revenue from data (email, text, and web browsing) growing sharply, while revenue from voice declined. Cingular needed a new vehicle to drive its growth.

After the launch of the iPod in 2002, Steve Jobs realized that it was only a matter of time before cell phones would make his innovation redundant.

Jobs approached Motorola to develop a handset that would work with his music store. In 2005, Jobs, along with Cingular, launched ROKR, a Motorola handset, but consumers rejected it. Jobs realized he would have to develop the phone himself. However, he had a problem. The carriers had become accustomed to treating their handset suppliers with disdain. Their strategy worked well when carriers were giving away cheap phones to sign up new customers, but when new customer growth declined, they needed something that would attract subscribers from the competition.

For his new phone, Jobs wanted flexibility and control, which was unheard of in the wireless industry in those days. He was looking to reinvent the time-consuming in-store sign-up process, and he was seeking complete control over the design, manufacture, and marketing of the iPhone.

He proposed a unique revenue-sharing model in which Apple would get $10 a month from every iPhone subscriber. In return, Jobs was willing to share 10% of iPhone's sales in carrier stores and a thin slice of Apple's iTunes revenue and was prepared to give the carrier five-year exclusivity. Additionally, Jobs was looking for complete secrecy until the launch of the new product. The carrier would have to take a risk based on Jobs's word only.

Verizon promptly turned Jobs down. Sigman, on the other hand, was willing to compromise and bet on Jobs. It took Sigman more than a year to get Cingular's board to approve the deal. Cingular risked turning its network into a conduit for content, or "dumb pipe" as Jobs called it, rather than a creator of content. Sigman was betting that the revenue from data traffic would more than make up for the drop in revenue from content.

Jobs launched the iPhone in January 2007, at a time when Verizon had just edged out Cingular as the number-one wireless carrier in the United States. But the consumer response was even more ecstatic than Jobs and Sigman had hoped.

Over the next five years, despite all the network challenges, AT&T Wireless regained and maintained its lead over Verizon. AT&T's data traffic grew 200 times over those years, and the average smartphone user spent twice as much as the voice user. The iPhone helped AT&T to achieve the fastest smartphone subscriber growth ever recorded until then, and AT&T's wireless profit margin jumped by 1.7%. This was during the Great Recession, when consumer spending on all other products was declining. Verizon later begged Apple to sell the iPhone to its subscribers after receiving constant pressure from its customers.

Cingular achieved excellence by partnering with Apple. It improved its network by expanding geographical coverage, increasing speed (3G, 4G, and LTE), and addressing bandwidth issues. It also improved the customer interface, the activation process, and the overall customer experience.

Cingular moved from the mentality of a monopoly to that of a customer-oriented services company. Both Cingular and Apple gained from the relationship, but Sigman's vision completely changed the wireless industry in the United States. Before 2007, the U.S. wireless industry lagged behind Japan and other Asian countries in innovation. Sigman opened the proprietary carrier network to innovation, and the United States is now the leading innovator of wireless content and services. Who could have imagined that U.S. residents could use a mobile passport app to submit custom forms when they returned home from a trip abroad? Some may argue that Apple benefited the most from the partnership. That may be true, but the impact of Sigman's vision will help AT&T Wireless far into the future.

OTHER EXAMPLES

Suppliers' contributions to excellence span many industries. For example, GE and Pratt and Whitney engines continue to make Western aircraft and airline industries more fuel efficient. Russian and Chinese aircraft manufacturers have struggled with engine design issues that limit their aircraft capabilities both in civilian and military applications.

Look at Microsoft and Intel's contribution to the PC industry. The combined contribution of these two suppliers made personal computers a reality, creating a multi-billion-dollar industry for companies like Dell, HP, and Lenovo.

Are there other examples that we could see in the future? Take the example of the self-driving car now being developed by Google and other firms. This vehicle could ultimately revolutionize the automotive and transportation industries. Unfortunately, Google hasn't been very open to collaboration with other companies, which has slowed down the introduction of a self-driving car and provided rivals an opportunity to catch up.

Example from a Less Strategic Area—Travel

In all these examples, visionary leaders made the change happen, and sourcing teams played a supporting role. Even on a smaller scale, sourcing teams can help their business teams achieve excellence. For example, the sourcing organization at a medical device company engaged our team to help it reduce its travel costs. The company was trying to integrate its European operations with its U.S. business under one management structure, and business travel from the United States was increasing.

A traditional sourcing approach would suggest that our team should have looked at different modes of travel and then negotiated with an individual provider to get better deals, thereby reducing costs. Also, the standard playbook would require that we put a travel policy in place that would make it difficult for travelers to use upgrades, force them to use cheaper hotels, and restrict their ability to spend. The logic was to implement controls and also to make the travel painful, so travelers would only travel when absolutely necessary.

We took an entirely different approach. Our team focused on understanding the needs for travel and finding a solution that would meet both the needs of the travelers and the business need to reduce costs. U.S. managers were traveling to meet with their counterparts in Europe to develop a relationship. Using a standard sourcing approach would build resentment within the U.S. team and ultimately undermine corporate objectives.

Our team looked at alternate ways for the U.S. team to meet with its European counterparts without having to travel. As we spent time brainstorming, we realized that the company had invested in a Cisco telepresence solution, which was just being introduced at that time.

The Cisco telepresence solution made virtual videoconferences possible. The utilization of these facilities at that time was low. I met with the president of the division impacted by the change and asked him to personally use the telepresence rooms and avoid travel as much as possible.

The logic was simple: His family and his team in the United States needed him at home. In six months, the company's travel fell by half, and the utilization of the telepresence room reached as high as 90%. The teams were happy, integration went smoothly, and travel costs went way down—even below the client's wildest dreams. Many companies have since taken this approach to reduce travel expenses.

The sourcing team drove excellence by understanding business goals and the travel needs of users, and then identifying alternate ways to achieve a better outcome. This means that the solution not only helped the business to reduce costs but also allowed for its end goal of business integration. This was completely different than the traditional sourcing approach and was facilitated by working with the business to define what an excellent outcome would look like.

INVOLVING SOURCING IN EXCELLENCE

Sometime in the 1990s, sourcing as a field of management evolved from issuing purchase orders (transaction management) to providing expertise on supply markets (category management). It moved from finalizing contracts once they were agreed upon by the business teams to developing a deep understanding of supply markets and facilitating the selection of suppliers. This had a tremendous impact on the way corporate leadership viewed sourcing professionals. Sourcing moved from finalizing pricing to managing third-party cost.

The next evolution of sourcing will probably see sourcing professionals contribute to business strategy more directly by moving from being a cost center to becoming a more integral part of the business, similar to marketing or the R&D organization.

What does that mean? Instead of just providing expertise about the supply side, the sourcing organization will start to collaborate with the business organization to drive excellence, a process that will start by jointly defining what excellence looks like before buying the solution from suppliers. Driving excellence will ensure that companies can compete effectively in the market, not only today but also in the future.

Sourcing processes currently start with the assumption that a business knows the solution it wants to buy. The sourcing team then finds the best supplier for the solution and strikes a deal. However, the fact is, most business organizations do not know what they need to compete in the future, so they end up providing only recent information to sourcing teams to base their procurement judgments upon. These solutions may not help companies compete effectively in the future, and the businesses end up working with the wrong suppliers and get stuck in deals that don't add value.

To drive excellence, the sourcing team needs to collaborate with the business organization early on to define what an excellent solution will look like in two to five years. Defining an excellent solution requires an open mind, good knowledge of the business, and collaboration with experts and suppliers to develop a solution that will help the business organization succeed in the long run. The sourcing team can bring in experts and suppliers to collaborate and help their business organizations define an excellent solution. Once the solution is defined, then the sourcing team can find the right suppliers and negotiate a contract that will be beneficial in the long run.

DEFINING EXCELLENCE

Everyone wants excellence, but few people know how to get there. There are several definitions of excellence. The standard definition is "the quality of being outstanding or extremely good." Some would say excellence is about being the very best. Unfortunately, most literature provides the elements of excellence but doesn't provide a path to achieving it. So excellence has remained a mostly theoretical concept, and companies struggle to make it tangible.

I define excellence for my clients as a state that is two to five years in the future and would make the client stand out against its competition. What is excellent for one company may not be excellent for others, and the future state should be uniquely tailored to the client's business model. This definition is more tangible as it provides a clear path toward excellence instead of just a vague idea. The definition also shows that the client cannot reach the end state by incremental improvement, and they have to make a significant, focused effort to get there.

A discussion about the future state typically makes most business executives reflect on their understanding of customer requirements and on what changes they anticipate in the business environment. Most would readily admit that their understanding of a potential future excellent state is limited, and they need help in defining it.

I have taken two approaches to helping my clients create a vision of excellence. One is based on the concept of "360 triangulation" and the second is based on supplier workshops. The choice of approach depends on who is responsible for managing the work.

If the client is managing the work internally with its own staff, then 360 triangulation is appropriate, whereas supplier workshops are most likely suitable for an outsourced environment or when a third party is responsible for managing the work. Involving suppliers in the process is critical. Sometimes, supplier involvement gets pushback from managers because they feel suppliers are not knowledgeable and may not have an adequate strategic perspective of the business. It is true that suppliers may lack strategic knowledge, but they work with other leading corporations and can provide unique insights that can help in defining the future state.

I will give two examples to explain the approaches—the first shows how to use 360 triangulation to better define a problem scenario, and the second brainstorms potential solutions for a decision already made by a client via supplier workshops.

360 TRIANGULATION

In this approach, the vision of excellence is developed by triangulating with customers, stakeholders, and suppliers—a view from all sides of the business. I have used this approach extensively, including at a leading coffee retailer and a financial services client. Both clients believed in excellence in everything they did. Any recommendation to them required sound logic, and they never accepted a solution because other companies in their industry were implementing it. They needed a unique and innovative approach that would work within their business model.

The 360 triangulation process uses five different sources of information to form the vision of the future, and then it validates them with a credible group of suppliers. Let me explain the process with an example from a coffee retailer where our team sourced cups for cold beverages.

Cold beverages were served in the summer months in plastic cups made out of PET, a compound that was as clear as glass. However, the suppliers' capacity was not keeping pace with the company's rapid growth, and there was a distinct risk that the retailer would run out of cups during peak summer demand. Suppliers were asking for a 40% to 50% price increase, as they were low on capacity. These cups were also not environmentally friendly because they were plastic, which is difficult to recycle and usually ends up in a landfill.

The client's sourcing organization hired us to source plastic cups. The sourcing team warned us that the client's leadership team was slow in making decisions. The summer season was 6 months away, and the leadership team had needed 12 months to come to a prior decision. There was a risk that the leadership team would not be able to come to an agreement to resolve supply problems for the summer. To find the best solution, we considered the following:

- **Stakeholder Interviews:** Marketing was a key stakeholder in the process of selecting plastic cups. They looked at the cups as a way to advertise the company's product. Interviews with the marketing team provided valuable insight into the constraints that we needed to take into consideration, such as the importance of having a glass-like appeal. The marketing organization essentially wanted us to find more suppliers that could provide PET cups.
- **Select Supplier Interviews:** These showed that the incumbent supplier, the largest in the industry, didn't have sufficient capacity. It had made a calculation error in estimating future demand. It had also committed its capacity to customers willing to pay higher prices than the client was willing to pay. Other suppliers in the market were running at high-capacity utilization and could only provide marginal volume at a very high price. It would take 12 to 24 months for suppliers to add any capacity.
- **Research:** New technologies were being introduced in the market. One particular technology got our attention. The suppliers were introducing a plastic resin called PP, for applications such as smaller water cups. This technology could be modified to make larger cold beverage cups. There was excess capacity in the market, and the cups took up less landfill space and were more environmentally friendly than PET. The suppliers could make the cups thinner, reducing plastic by 30%. The challenge was that PP cups were not as transparent as PET cups and, therefore, not as attractive.

- **Voice of the Customer:** The marketing team didn't support PP cups because they were not as transparent as PET cups. They also felt that the PP cups were a little flimsy. But the cups were not flimsy when filled with a cold beverage or even water. To test whether the cups would be accepted by consumers, our team made samples and sent them to stores for comments. We provided a side-by-side comparison with PET cups and asked for feedback. Store employees loved the environmentally friendlier concept of PP cups, and they believed that transparency was not an issue. In any case, when beverages were served in the PET cups, dark beverages blocked transparency in those cups, too.

- **Expert Opinion:** This was helpful in understanding future trends in plastic containers and food safety issues with PP cups. The PP cups were made from FDA-certified food-grade plastics. Experts were completely supportive of the PP cups as they contained fewer harmful ingredients. They suggested that PET availability was likely to remain tight for many years, because the capacity of plastic manufacturing upstream was constrained. The client could pay higher prices to get the supplies as a short-term fix, but they would have difficulty in sustaining this.

The 360 triangulation process showed that our team could buy PET capacity to get through the summer demand but that it was not a sustainable solution. A better solution would be to move to PP cups. Since the marketing organization was not in support of such a move, it was decided to bring the issue to the attention of the founder, who usually didn't get involved in operational issues and took a long time to mediate any major debates.

Our team provided all the data on PP and PET cups for the founder's review. The founder loved the PP cups, not because they were cheaper, but because of the environmentally friendly story. He realized PP cups were still plastic cups, but it was a step in the right direction. Being environmentally friendly was core to this retailer's philosophy. He did not want to hide the fact that the company was moving to a different plastic product. Instead, he asked the marketing team to advertise it in bold words and ensure that consumers knew about this change in the interest of the environment.

The cups were introduced in a phased manner to manage the risk of consumer rejection. The consumers loved the concept and appreciated the company's efforts to respect the environment. Even today, several years after they were introduced, the PP cups are still being used at retail stores across the country.

The 360 triangulation process worked well in this case because the change on the supplier side was relatively simple (moving from one plastic product to another), whereas the potential impact on the client's end was huge. The sourcing organization on its own couldn't have been able to make this choice. It was essential that all organizations that were involved in customer management (store employees, marketing team, and leadership team) brought into the decision and made ready to execute the plan.

SUPPLIER WORKSHOPS

Our team was engaged by a financial services firm in the New York area to source its food service providers. While it might not appear critical from a bottom-line perspective, the head of the institution was personally focused on food sourcing because of its link to employee satisfaction and retention. The client catered food for its five offices from different local restaurants. Each location had multiple pantries serving coffee, tea, and snacks, and a provider managed it. Food was provided free to all employees. Lunch was catered from local restaurants, which provided variety but inconsistent quality and rapidly increasing costs.

After reviewing best practices in the market, we recommended the client outsource food services to one provider to simplify the process.

This provider could choose to do the work either in-house or to buy from restaurants. We decided to use a supplier workshop approach to create a vision for the excellent state before sourcing. We scheduled two workshops to design the future state:

- **Workshop 1—Supplier Review of Current State:** The objective of the first workshop was to provide suppliers with a deeper understanding of the client's current state. The suppliers were also provided with site tours.

  Four suppliers were selected to develop the future food-outsourcing model. The research showed that new suppliers were getting into the market and had started providing innovative restaurant-quality menus to corporate clients. Of the four suppliers selected by our team, two were traditional food providers, and two were the new-generation suppliers.

  The suppliers were provided with a current portfolio consisting of costs and business strategy information, along with current challenges. After Workshop 1, suppliers were asked to provide a written proposal with their proposed solution along with pricing guidance. Suppliers were encouraged to propose multiple solutions.

- **Workshop 2—Solution Development:** The second workshop was a working session where the client and supplier teams worked together to assess the viability of each of the suppliers' proposed solutions. From the client's perspective, this workshop helped clarify different solutions that could potentially lead to an excellent result. From the suppliers' perspective, the workshop provided an opportunity to gather feedback from the client team that would help them refine their thinking.

  Each supplier proposed a different model for the future of the outsourced environment. As we discussed matters with the suppliers, our team realized that the food-catering business is changing. Instead of having cafeterias at every location, it made sense to have one central kitchen from which the food for all of the different office locations could be catered. In this way, food production would be consistent and would also be out of sight. It showed that the contracting model was changing from a markup-based approach, where suppliers make a profit margin on food products, to a transparent cost pass-through approach, with agreed-upon margins.

After Workshop 2, the client team gathered to critique the various solutions proposed by the suppliers. The team particularly liked the idea of outsourcing to one provider who would make the food in-house at a central kitchen. It would provide fresh food, consistent quality, and reduced costs. The approach also envisioned the provider sourcing some popular ethnic menus from local restaurants.

The solution selected by the client team was radically different from the solution used by other financial services companies in the New York area. The popular model was to select a cafeteria provider and menu based on food preferences at an office location. None of the food was freshly made except for some comfort food like burgers or hot dogs. The client's decision to cater food was a radical departure, which made complete sense in its situation.

Once the solution was selected, it was then broached with different stakeholders and the leadership team for feedback and refinement. The process involved significant engagement with suppliers and resulted in a solution that was considered excellent by everyone involved, including the suppliers. The solution energized the client team and encouraged them to start moving in a direction they felt made them significantly more efficient in their asset utilization.

SOURCING EXCELLENT SOLUTIONS

After the final solution was agreed to by the client team, the next step was to select the right supplier and to arrange a contract. Learning from our previous experience that selecting the right supplier is not sufficient, we needed to select the right supplier team to achieve excellent outcomes. Typically, suppliers would bring a group of individuals during the selection process, but they would switch the members after they were awarded the business. We needed a team that could not only work well with the client's culture but also had the capability to guide the client toward the best solution. It was emphasized that the business award was contingent on the client's comfort as well as its involvement in the selection of the supplier members who would work with the client team on a day-to-day basis.

Supplier Selection

An RFP was provided to suppliers for their final proposal, with the emphasis on a team that would work well with the client's culture. Once the client reviewed the proposal, we scheduled a workshop so the client team could develop a deeper understanding of each of the supplier proposals. The workshop also allowed suppliers to get final feedback from the client team.

After the workshop, the suppliers were asked to refine and send their final proposals for consideration. At this time, the client team selected the supplier they felt would be most capable of delivering the best solution as well as the right team. The next step was to specifically select the members of the supplier's team.

Selection of Supplier Team

When we started with interviews to select the supplier team, we soon realized that we were encountering interview bias. For example, we were selecting team members who reflected the views of the interviewers instead of selecting the execution team required to perform the job. To avoid interview bias, we shifted to selecting the supplier team through personality tests.

Pricing and Service-Level Negotiations

By the time we were ready for negotiations about price, the client team ended up with a rich collection of cost data. Should-cost modeling was particularly helpful because buying customized solutions made financial comparison and negotiation with the selected supplier much more challenging.

We took an open-book approach while negotiating with the supplier, so any error in assumptions could be corrected. Once the pricing was finalized, the service-level agreements and related incentives and penalties were agreed upon. Most of these were proposed by the supplier during the solution development, so reaching an agreement was fairly easy and quick.

The traditional sourcing approach is where the business has a product or service in mind and then selects between what's offered by various suppliers and contracts with the most suitable supplier. In contrast, the approach used by our team focused on identifying the most excellent solution for the business, finding the right supplier, choosing its team, and then contracting. This ensured that clients had a sourcing solution that was appropriate for their business for many years in the future, that the suppliers were capable of delivering the solution, and that there was a clear path to excellence.

In both of the examples above, the client ended up using the selected solution over a long period. These solutions clearly helped the client stand out from the competition and drove their businesses to excellence.

MAKING EXCELLENCE A REALITY

Excellence is not just a utopia; it can be achieved. But companies cannot achieve excellence without including their partners and suppliers. With more and more work being performed by suppliers, who at times are more aware of innovative solutions, it is critical that sourcing teams are able to draw on suppliers' expertise to drive excellence.

Sourcing teams have to define the ideal end state in collaboration with their business partners. They can define the state of excellence via 360 triangulation or supplier workshops. Both require the involvement of suppliers.

After an ideal end state is defined, sourcing organizations have a critical role to play in achieving it. There is a need to rethink the standard sourcing process. The assumption has been that businesses know what solutions to buy, and therefore the focus is on supplier selection and contracting. But that assumption is no longer valid, and sourcing processes need to be updated to reflect the approach suggested in this chapter. To accomplish these goals, a high level of cost analysis becomes useful because as suppliers propose different solutions apples-to-apples comparisons become more difficult. Expertise on should-cost modeling becomes much more critical to not only developing the initial solution but also to updating it as things change postcontract.

CONCLUSION

AS I HAVE WRITTEN THROUGHOUT THIS book, an effective supply chain and sourcing organization can help management find a competitive advantage. This often translates directly into healthy growth and a stronger bottom line. There is, however, a caveat to this new approach: If implemented improperly, a company can wind up with a real hangover.

HP'S STRUGGLE

Take, for example, HP's struggle in the PC industry. In an effort to compete with its main rival, Dell, Carly Fiorina merged HP with Compaq in 2001. She believed the acquisition would provide significant cost savings to the merged firm by removing redundant administrative functions. HP would achieve sufficient scale to compete effectively with Dell.

However, Fiorina's strategy ignored the fact that Dell had a superlative approach to its supply chain, and achieving efficiency alone would not make HP competitive in the long run.

What was missing? HP needed to boost revenue by the introduction of newer-generation products that could be put in consumers' hands quickly at an affordable price. Fiorina was a great visionary and marketing person, but she lacked operational skills. She struggled with the integration, created significant organizational backlash, and conceded a valuable time advantage to Dell and Apple.

In 2005, Mark Hurd, an operation-focused CEO, was hired by HP to fix the integration. Hurd reduced the workforce and consolidated infrastructure to reduce costs. He also disbanded HP's centralized supply chain in favor of one that was decentralized—a strategy that focused on tailoring supply chains by business unit.

He focused on using the sourcing and supply chain organizations to drive efficiency. Also, he started investing in a direct-to-consumer distribution by debottlenecking the supply chain, a topic I explored in Chapter 4. These were the first steps to getting the supply chain and sourcing organizations to contribute to the overall success of the company.

The draconian measures paid off, and HP's profit margins improved, allowing it to expand via still more acquisitions. Hurd advanced product lines, but innovation never kept pace with changing market demands. HP never moved past its focus on supply-side cost reduction to develop a competitive edge. The IT market became disrupted as demand moved from PCs to tablets and enterprise software to apps, eventually driving down HP's revenue and profitability.

HP failed to a large extent because its leaders believed that old business strategies—incremental product innovation, acquisitions, and efficiency—could somehow make it a successful company. Even Dell suffered from the same mindset, despite having significant prowess with supply chain. A better approach would have been to focus on growth through alliances, customer satisfaction, and speeding the company's responsiveness to market demand with help from the supply chain and sourcing.

Similar challenges are visible in other diversified corporations and industries, including such nonmanufacturing examples as the private equity (PE) industry.

PRIVATE EQUITY INDUSTRY CHALLENGES

The PE industry went through a period of disruption that required assets to be held for a longer period of time. The biggest challenge for the industry was to extract value from operational stuff, such as the supply chain and sourcing organization at acquired firms, a challenge it had not previously had to address.

Indeed, some PE firms even started hiring "operating partners" who had a background in supply chains and sourcing. Unfortunately, PE still worked primarily from a cost-reduction perspective, meaning management had a short-term focus on profitability that did not confer a sustained competitive advantage. Similar to the strategy taken by HP, companies owned by PE firms tended to focus on reducing head count, on beating suppliers down to reduce costs, and on reducing investment in infrastructure.

For example, 3G Capital, a private equity PE firm founded by five Brazilian investors, was hailed for its focus on operational improvement. Its approach was very similar to the one used by HP—head count reduction to improve margins, with the savings being used to buy other companies.

3G Capital bought Burger King in 2010 and focused on cutting head count to increase profit margins. Once the margin improved, the cash flow provided leverage to buy Canada's Tim Hortons and then to buy U.S. food group Kraft in partnership with Warren Buffett. It then merged Kraft with H.J. Heinz.

Though 3G Capital was changing the paradigm in PE by focusing on operations, it has not tapped the full potential benefits available in the supply chain and sourcing areas.

SUSTAINABLE COMPETITIVE ADVANTAGE FOR DIVERSIFIED COMPANIES

Focusing on efficiency does not provide a sustainable competitive advantage on its own. To reap the full benefit from improvements to supply chains and sourcing, companies have to reduce their business risks (overhead), and then create a better way to respond to customers. It could be through better customer service, expansion of service through alliances, or faster response to changing demand. If the food industry gets disrupted by new business models, 3G Capital will probably find that the lack of capabilities in its supply chain and sourcing organizations has become its Achilles' heel.

How can diversified companies capture value from operations? By applying the following approaches suggested in this book:

- The first thing to do is to recognize that there is value in looking at operations across the company's whole portfolio, instead of separately examining individual business units. Many diversified companies have the mindset that each business unit CEO is an entrepreneur and that he or she should have the full freedom of running his or her operations. A centralized supply chain and sourcing organization is looked at as a hindrance to the operational flexibility of business unit leaders. We recommend forming a center of excellence to leverage volume across business units to reduce costs, while not hindering business units' ability to execute.

  A center of excellence determines policies and procedures, provides guidelines, selects vendors for different types of work, and negotiates prices and contracts. Business unit leaders still have the complete freedom to choose the provider and type of work to be performed based on their individual requirements.

  Increased volume can provide efficient ways of buying and moving materials. Chapters 6 and 7 include examples of how diversified companies can use sourcing organizations to reduce costs for different services, such as marketing, outsourcing, and real estate, which are areas that are often overlooked. Collaboration among business units can reduce service costs.

- The second step is to reduce business risks through efficient operations. Finding ways to reduce operational risk and overhead costs can increase survivability when the market gets disrupted. Many companies suffer from supply chain bottlenecks and fail to respond to market changes quickly enough.

  Bottlenecks can happen either inside the company or at the

supplier's end. An effort to reduce bottlenecks can improve success when businesses need to change direction. Similarly, companies make longer-term investments in infrastructure, whether it is IT, inventory, or fixed overheads. These investments need to be made in a smart way to ensure that they do not drag companies to bankruptcy when demand changes direction. Chapters 4 and 5 provide ideas on how to reduce overhead costs and supply chain bottlenecks. Diversified companies will be well served if they develop capabilities for managing operational risk centrally. This is essential to their ability to drive value.

The third step is to increase revenue. You cannot improve long-term business success by cutting costs alone. Improving customer service, finding ways to boost revenue, and amplifying alliance performance can help. Customer service can be improved without breaking the bank by tailoring service levels to the individual customer segment. This can be achieved by developing a menu of service levels appropriate for different segments. Additionally, companies should develop a service model that is difficult for the competition to match, then price it appropriately and find a way for customers to pay for the increased service.

Similarly, supply chains can help companies achieve their revenue targets by continuing to respond to market demand quickly. This can be accomplished by separating the supply chain by demand patterns, simplifying supplier networks, storing inventory strategically, negotiating flexible terms with suppliers, and allowing market demand to pull the products from factories.

Alliances can help companies achieve success in the market through transparent deal negotiation and effective ongoing relationship management. Chapters 1, 2, and 3 provide examples and approaches that can be used.

■ The fourth step is to drive business excellence. Chapter 8 shows how sourcing professionals can help management define excellence and pick the right partners—those best equipped to advance management's agenda. To drive excellence, sourcing teams need to collaborate with management to define what an excellent solution will look like two to five years ahead. Once the solution is defined, the sourcing team can find the right suppliers and negotiate a contract that will be beneficial in the long run.

IMPROVING LIVES

This book has focused primarily on the potential contribution supply chains and sourcing organizations can make to their companies' success. What's not covered are the social responsibilities of these organizations.

Clearly, these organizations have a responsibility toward sustainability and need to be environmentally conscious in everything they do. Recycling and reducing waste are commonsense goals that should be incorporated in any supply chain and sourcing strategy. A lot has been written about ethical sourcing. A sourcing organization has the responsibility to buy products from suppliers that treat workers well, pay fair wages, and use safe facilities. It is also important to avoid illegal trade of animals and plants. These social responsibilities should be ingrained in supply chain and sourcing organizations. They are the eyes and ears of their company as they work with outside providers. As such, they can help senior management to make more responsible choices.

Supply chain and sourcing professionals can help solve significant problems facing humanity. For example, it is estimated that 40% to 50% of world food production is wasted, and we have millions of people who go hungry all around the world. The problem is complex and becoming acute, but it's a supply chain problem. The food industry has the responsibility to reduce waste, whether it's in the company's control, the supplier's control, or the customer's control. Supply chain professionals should take up these social causes and provide solutions so we can leave a better world for our kids and grandkids.

A FINAL WORD

A MORE AGGRESSIVE MANAGEMENT APPROACH to supply chains and sourcing can provide a competitive edge in the disruptive and fiercely competitive business world that most firms face in today's market. Some CEOs and senior management leaders are starting to understand this, but few are instituting systemic and sustainable transformation. When senior management changes, too often the initiatives die, and organizations go back to where they were before.

Change is sustainable if it is demanded and nurtured from the top. I hope CEOs who read this book will now call upon their supply chain and sourcing organizations for help with business strategy. To do so will require an open mind and a willingness to depart from past practice. CEOs must also realize that their supply chain and sourcing organizations have not been trained to step out of their functional silos, and it will take time for them to begin to contribute. A patient approach is necessary to help transform these organizations.

A good example is Stefan Larsson, CEO of Ralph Lauren, who chose to make supply chains and sourcing his top focus. His Way Forward Plan included four "engines" to drive profitability and growth. These were broadening product variety, creating a demand-driven supply chain, achieving best-in-class sourcing, and implementing a multichannel distribution strategy (both online and brick and mortar). Three of the four engines focused on supply chain and sourcing areas. The key to the turnaround was improving supply chain speed from 15 months to 9 months, which was still far longer than Zara's 10–15 days discussed in the Foreword.

To plan inventory based on demand, Larsson introduced an eight-week test pipeline to identify winning merchandise to focus on for inventory buildup. Regarding sourcing, Larsson said he wanted Ralph

Lauren to collaborate with its supplier base in Asia, buying a large quantity of fabric for "icon" products depending on demand and reducing order quantity. Sourcing's objective should be to drive costs down while improving quality. The distribution strategy, on the other hand, should align with consumer demand from different channels by efficiently servicing online orders.

It's amazing to hear that a CEO is asking his supply chain and sourcing organization to step up and help the company win in the market. The steps highlighted by Larsson are clear and achievable. Though Larsson's plan will improve Ralph Lauren's performance, it's unlikely to provide the company a competitive edge. It is more of a catch-up plan. The next step will be to develop a plan that will provide a competitive advantage for Ralph Lauren—a plan unique to its business model.

Similarly, change will not be possible unless and until leaders of supply chain and sourcing organizations are willing to step out of their comfort zones. That means they must become intimately familiar with all aspects of the business, relying more on analytical tools than on past experience, focusing on collaboration with internal organizations and suppliers, and changing old practices. In each chapter of this book, I have shared ways to do things differently. Embracing these new approaches will be the first step.

Most supply chain and sourcing leaders are trained to be risk averse. Years of experience have taught them that their failure is highly visible and newsworthy, whereas their successes are buried deep inside financial statements. To help supply chain and sourcing organizations step out of their comfort zones, incentives will have to be changed. The right incentives will drive the correct behavior.

The state of the art in supply chain management and sourcing has not changed in a troublingly long time. This book offers the tools necessary for your organization to realize its full potential and for you to contribute fully to the success of your company.

GLOSSARY

Account Management: Management of sales and relationships with particular customers so that they will continue doing business with the company.

Ad Placement: Placement or positioning of an ad at the right location in newspaper, television, or online to avoid confusing its message.

Alliance: An agreement between two companies to achieve a common objective. The alliance could be for marketing a new product, joint product innovation, revenue growth, market share, new customer acquisitions, etc. Alliances are different from customer-supplier relationships where companies do not share common objectives.

Back Order: Items that could not be shipped for an order due to stock shortages.

Big Data: Analysis of the large volume of data being collected by companies through the point of sale or other IT systems.

Bottleneck: Constraint or obstacle that limits the ability to achieve full potential.

Brand Equity: Commercial value of a brand as compared to its generic equivalent.

Brief: A summary document that provides information about the expectations of all parties associated with an advertising campaign. For the client, it lays out services included and timing, while for the advertising firm, it specifies the revenues to be received for the campaign and what the firm needs to do to fulfill the agreement.

Campaign: Group of coordinated advertising messages that are similar in nature and placed in different types of media at fixed times. Apple's "Mac vs. PC" with 66 commercials would be an example of an advertising campaign.

Capacity: Maximum output or production ability of a machine, person, process, factory, product, or service.

Categories: Group of commodities that are similar or have similar supply markets.

Center of Excellence: A group that provides expertise or leadership in a particular area. The group could develop best practices, provide guidance, do research, and provide support and training to the user organizations. Center of Excellence success is measured by its ability to influence user groups to achieve an outcome rather than its ability to execute.

Change Management: An organized educational campaign to help teams change their approach, direction, or modes of operation. The objective of change management is to address concerns and reduce organizational pushback to a new way of doing things. Change management involves understanding stakeholder concerns, targeted communication, and talent management.

Channel: Method for a business to dispense its products or services, such as retail locations, web-based stores, call centers, or smartphones.

Commercial Printing: Process of taking a design from artwork and transferring that work onto a piece of paper or card stock. An example would be offset printing.

Commodities: Fungible raw materials such as metals (e.g., gold or silver), agricultural products (e.g., sugar), chemicals, or even services categorized for procurement purposes. A commodity typically involves a large group of sellers that sell similar products or services and buyers that buy similar products or services. The United Nations

Standard Products and Services Code (UNSPSC) provides a comprehensive commodity classification.

Community Affairs: Serves as a link between the company and the community as a whole. It promotes the organization's vision, message, expertise, and services and helps residents and organizations to connect.

Competitive Advantage: Refers to unique skill or ability that allows a company to attract customers better than the competition. A competitive advantage could be superior product performance, better quality, higher service, or lower cost. It depends on the need of the customers.

Contract Manufacturing: Manufacturing of products by a third party on behalf of a company. For example, Foxconn is a contract manufacturer of iPhone for Apple.

Cost Drivers: Underlying factors that cause a change in the cost of an activity.

Cost Model: A mathematical model that estimates the cost of a product or service. It involves identifying different cost elements, and then estimating overall cost by summing up those elements.

Cost Plus: A type of contract that pays for cost and additional profit to a vendor. It is meant to reduce financial risk for the vendor.

Cost Reduction: A process of reducing overall cost by removing unwanted expenses, simplifying work processes, or other strategies appropriate for a company's products or services.

Cost Savings: Measures reduction in expenses in a specified area. These areas are typically agreed upon contractually by the client and suppliers or outsource providers.

Creative Services: A team in the marketing organization that does creative work, such as writing, designing, and production.

Cross Sell: Practice of attempting to sell additional products to a customer during a sales call.

Customer Management: Practices to engage customers on a day-to-day basis. It could include managing expectations, product replenishment, reporting, billing, and other hands-on services.

Customer Satisfaction: Measures the ability of a company to meet or exceed customer expectations.

Customer Segmentation: Grouping customers for marketing purposes, based on criteria such as age, gender, interests, and spending habits.

Customer Service: Measures the quality of employee interaction with customers during and after the sales process. Elements of customer service may include quicker response to customer queries, easy return policy, speed in addressing concerns, etc.

Customization: Modifying products or services to meet each customer's requirement. Increased customization leads to greater variety and complexity in the supply chain.

Cycle Time: Total time from the start to the end of the process—time taken to complete one cycle of the operation. It includes work time, process time, and wait time, among other things.

Dashboard: Tool that summarizes key performance indicators/metrics. It is easy to read and usually has red, yellow, and green indicators to flag when a company is or is not meeting its targets.

Data Companies: Companies that collect point-of-sale data or consumer buying data and sell this data to other businesses.

Debottleneck: Act of removing the constraint or obstacle that limits performance or achievement of full potential.

Defect Rate: Percentage of products or services that do not meet the required quality or specifications.

Demand: Signal from a consumer or customer that they will consume a product or service. An example is a consumer buying a product at a store.

Demand Fluctuation: Upward or downward movement of demand due to external factors such as sales promotion, competitor promotion, seasonality, and fashion trends.

Demand Planning: A step in the sales & operations planning (S&OP) process that identifies the underlying source of demand and its trends. The demand-planning process is used to refine the sales forecast.

Depot: Small warehouse to store products in a remote location.

Design: First step in the construction of a new product or service. It is a creative process that tries to meet the customer requirements better than the competition. A company's design philosophy could significantly influence supply chain and manufacturing complexity.

Digital Media: Refers to computer programs, software, digital imagery, digital video, video games, web pages, websites, etc., which can be accessed by computers or electronic devices. This is different from print media, such as printed books, newspapers and magazines, and other traditional media.

Direct Cost: Cost, such as material or labor, that can be attributed to the production of particular goods or services.

Direct Delivery: Process of shipping from a manufacturing plant or distribution center to the consumer, thus bypassing retail stores.

Direct Marketing: Selling products or services directly to the end user through mail or digital media order or telephone rather than advertising through television to a large population.

Disintermediation: Removal of a middleman or agent between a provider and end user. In this book, it means removal of an outsourcing provider between customer and suppliers.

Distribution: Activities associated with the movement of material, usually finished goods or services, from the plant to the customer. These activities encompass areas such as transportation, warehousing, material handling, order management, and repackaging.

Distribution Center: Warehouse where inventory is held from manufacturing pending distribution to the customers.

Distributor: An agent who supplies goods to stores and other businesses from a manufacturer.

Economy of Scale, or Scale: A concept dating back to Adam Smith that states that an entity will reduce cost per unit of output as it gains size (scale). Two drivers of cost reduction are fixed costs getting spread over a larger number of units and the ability of the provider to utilize better production technology. There is a limit to the economy of scale. Beyond a certain size, the cost per additional unit begins to increase due to increased complexity of operation.

Effectiveness: The degree to which end objectives are achieved.

Efficiency: Measure of how much money or resources are used to achieve the end goals.

Engineering: The science of making a product or service from design.

Error Rate: Percentage of tasks that are inaccurately performed.

Ethical Sourcing: A process where the buyer ensures that the products being sourced are produced in a safe facility, the workers are treated well and paid fairly, and the supplier is environmentally responsible. These are the concerns typically but not solely arising from third-world countries where country regulations are not strong and don't protect workers or the environment.

Excellence: Refers to service or quality that far surpasses accepted norms and sets a higher bar for all providers of that product or service.

Expediting: A process to speed up work, shipment, or production.

Explainer Video: A short animated video used by businesses to tell their brands' stories.

Facilities Management: A broad range of services provided for the smooth functioning of the work environment for occupants of a building or facility. These services could be provided by in-house resources, an outsource provider, or third parties. Depending on the facility, the services may include maintenance, cleaning, security, safety, heating and air-conditioning, food, etc.

Fast Moving: Product or service that has regular demand.

Fixed Price: A type of contract where a set payment amount is agreed upon for a particular job. The provider takes the risk of controlling cost. It gets paid the same amount irrespective of the actual cost.

Flexibility: Ability to respond quickly and efficiently to changing demands.

Focus Group: Marketing technique that uses a small group of end users to glean insights into consumer reaction to a product or service changes.

Forecast: Estimate of future demand based on historical data by using different statistical techniques.

General Ledger (GL): Book of accounts that records all transactions related to a company's assets, liabilities, revenue, and expenses. It is a central repository for all accounting data.

Glide Path: A contract clause that provides an agreed-upon path for cost reduction. For example, a clause in a five-year outsourcing contract may suggest 5% year-over-year cost reduction for the first two years and then 10% year-over-year reduction for the next three years.

Globalization: Refers to trade and movement of goods and services across international borders. It is a process facilitated by trade agreements and information technology.

Governance: A process of managing cross-functional projects where there is no apparent single owner. The process lays out policy and procedures, reporting, and escalation of issues for quicker resolution.

Government Accountability Office (GAO): U.S. government agency that provides auditing, evaluation, and investigative services for the U.S. Congress.

Ground-Up Production: A production process that starts from scratch instead of preassembled parts. This manufacturing process is laborious but appropriate for smaller-quantity high-performance items such as vehicles, as it allows fine-tuning of each component for overall performance.

Guaranteed Maximum Price (GMP): A modified cost-plus contract where a provider is paid cost and profit subject to a ceiling. Beyond the limit, the provider is responsible for the cost. GMP allows for shared financial risk with the provider.

Handyman Services: Refers to a broad range of repairs around the home or office. These tasks may include small repair and maintenance work, which are considered odd jobs and don't particularly require a skilled contractor.

Hard Services: Industry term for construction-related activities such as office remodeling, building maintenance, heating and air-conditioning services, equipment maintenance, etc. Most of these services are facility related.

Incentives: Financial or nonfinancial inducements that influence the behavior of a person or a group.

Indirect Costs: Costs such as depreciation or administrative expenses that are allocated to multiple goods or services.

Influencing Skills: The ability to persuade others or negotiate to reach an agreement.

Innovation: Creating or developing a new product, idea, or method that meets the existing or future needs of consumers or end users.

Integrated Facilities Management (IFM): An outsourcing provider that provides services across diverse areas such as project management, landscaping, construction, janitorial, food services, and energy management. IFM brings both hard (construction-related) and soft (day-to-day employee) services under the management of one outsource provider.

This follows the concept of "one throat to choke." The IFM provider may not provide all the services with in-house resources but can hire or work with third parties to provide the complete suite of services.

Inventory: Material that is held in anticipation of a customer order.

Inventory Management: Process of ensuring the availability of material when customer orders are received while avoiding excess or nonmoving inventory.

Inventory Planning: Process of balancing inventory and customer service levels throughout the supply chain.

Inventory Turn: Measure of how many times a company's inventory has been sold during a period of time. The faster the turn, the lower the cash tied up in inventory.

Key Performance Indicators (KPIs): A mathematical formula to measure the performance of an important business function or area. It helps management understand how effectively business objectives are being achieved.

Lead Time: Total time between order placement and receipt by the customer. It involves order processing, production, shipment, and transit.

Logistics: The management of the flow of material from one point to another. The process involves material handling, transportation, and inventory management. In some cases, it may involve information flow, production, warehousing, and security.

Management Fee: A fee charged by an outsourcing company to provide oversight of its employees and third-party providers. It includes both profit margin and a fee to compensate for coordination and supplier management.

Market Research: The process of identifying and analyzing market need, market size, competition, etc., to provide valuable information.

Matrix Organization: Organization where a person may report to multiple managers.

Media: Means of mass communication such as television, radio, newspapers, and the Internet.

Metrics: Method to quantify the work performed in an activity. The best ones are designed to promote desired employee behavior.

Modeling: Process of applying mathematics to a real-world problem intended to increase understanding of the process.

Modular Design: A philosophy that divides a complex design into smaller modules that could be independently manufactured and used in different systems. The concept is regularly applied in the manufacturing of computers, cars, electronic equipment, and others. Modular design combines the advantages of standardization with customization. A new product may have some standard modules (like a power system) and may have new modules tailored to specific customer requirements.

Network: Path for movement of goods or information.

Nonmoving Inventory: Inventory for which there is no demand.

Offshoring: The practice of moving processes or services overseas to take advantage of lower labor or other costs such as energy, land cost, etc.

Online Advertising: A form of advertising that uses the Internet to deliver marketing messages to end users.

Operations: Refers to organizations such as manufacturing, supply chain, sourcing, transportation, warehousing, quality, and others.

Order Backlog: Sales order that is pending and needs to be fulfilled. Typically happens when capacity is not adequate to meet the customer order, and the customer has to wait to receive their deliveries.

Organizational Silo: An organization with rigid boundaries and/or processes that does not interact well with other organizations to achieve overall goals of the company.

Outdoor Advertising: Advertising on billboards; bus benches; interiors and exteriors of buses, taxis, trucks, and other locations.

Outsourcing: The practice of using an outside provider to perform activities that are traditionally handled by internal staff and resources. The work can involve day-to-day unplanned management tasks as well as discrete services.

Partner Management: Management of day-to-day relationships with business partners.

Penalty: Negative incentive to stop a particular behavior. Typically, a contract with suppliers may have a penalty associated with performance falling below a certain threshold. The penalty could be monetary or nonmonetary in nature.

Perfect Order: Order that has met all requirements, such as order quantity, timeliness, quality, and documentation.

Point-of-Sale Marketing: Refers to all efforts that increase sales at a cash register. For example, at supermarkets, it is common to find candy bars, magazines, water, and other items close to the cash register.

Price Promotion: Refers to price discount offered to consumers to increase sales volume. Discounts offered during Christmas or other holidays by retailers are considered to be price promotions. Other examples are coupons, two-for-one offers, and temporary price cuts.

Print: Advertising in newspaper and magazines.

Print Production: Industrial and commercial processes of printing.

Private Equity (PE): Refers to a fund that is raised from private investors. In this book, it refers to investments made by these funds in distressed companies. The companies invested in by the industry are not publicly traded, which allows the PE company to fix longer-term problems.

Product Development: An organization that develops and brings new products to market.

Product Differentiation: A process of distinguishing a product or service from other similar products or services in the market. The distinction could be based on performance, quality, aesthetics, or other factors that are important to end users.

Production Downtime: Time during which a machine or process cannot be utilized.

Production Size: Sometimes referred to as lot size. Production processes require a minimum volume to get to the lowest unit cost. Producing below the minimum volume will increase cost as initial wastages and downtime get allocated to the smaller volume. For some production processes, there may not be a choice to produce the minimum volume in order to make the production run.

Productivity: Measure of the efficiency of resource utilization.

Promotion: Raising customer awareness of a product or brand.

Proxy: A substitute used in modeling in the place of actual data. This may be because actual data is not available or difficult to get. A proxy has to reflect the characteristics of the actual data and therefore can be taken as a substitute. For example, you may not know actual foot traffic in a Walmart store, but the cars parked in front of the store could act as a substitute in estimating foot traffic.

Publicity: Gaining public awareness or visibility for a product or service.

Public Relations: Ongoing communications to maintain a strong public image of a company, product, or person through different media such as newspapers, television, magazines, etc., without making a direct payment. An example of public relations would be generating an interview with a television anchor, rather than paying to advertise the message.

Pull-Based: In a pull-based system, actual customer orders drive activity in the supply chain. For example, once a product is sold, the store orders the exact quantity of the product sold from the warehouse, then the warehouse orders from the plant, and the plant orders from the suppliers. There is no artificial tinkering with the order quantity while it gets moved through different participants in the supply chain.

Push: Process of sending products to distribution centers and retailers without receiving any information about demand.

Qualitative Method: Often part of survey methodology, including telephone and consumer satisfaction surveys. The objective is to examine the why and how of decision making.

Quantitative Techniques: Gathering and statistical analysis of data leading to business decisions.

Real Estate Services: A broad range of services involved in managing properties consisting of land or buildings. It involves buying, selling, or renting, along with construction and maintenance of properties.

Replenishment: Process of moving or resupplying inventory from one warehouse to another location.

Response Time: Time taken to respond to an order or a request for service. Typically, a response time includes wait time for the order in the queue, process time, and then transmission time.

Retail Stocks: Inventory that is held by retailers in addition to inventory maintained by a company.

Reverse Logistics: Refers to logistics associated with products that are returned. The process involves refurbishing the product for reuse or proper disposal.

ROI: Return on investment measures profit as a percentage of investment.

Sales Commission, or Commission: A commission is an additional compensation paid to a salesperson for achieving or exceeding a sales target. The objective is to motivate sales agents to sell more to customers. Sometimes commissions make salespeople too aggressive.

Sales Promotion: Sales tactic to create consumer excitement to buy products or services.

Service-Level Agreements (SLAs): Translation of customer need in simple work outputs. For example, a customer need could be prompt response during the service outage. The SLA could be an agreement to respond to a customer concern within the hour and fix the problem within 24 hours.

Service Model: A process for servicing customer requirements. For example, a service model for a delivery person may include checking a vehicle in the morning, loading the vehicle, making deliveries during the day, returning an inventory of deliveries that could not be made, and returning and reporting any problem with the vehicle.

Shared Services: A way to organize administrative functions in one central organization, so these services can be provided consistently and cost-effectively across all business units. Administrative functions include accounting, human resources, facilities management, procurement, and others.

Should-Cost: An estimated cost of a product or service when produced under normal circumstances.

Simulation: Artificial way of creating a real-life situation through designing a model, executing the model on a digital computer, and analyzing the output.

Slow Moving: Product that has sporadic demand.

Soft Services: Industry term for day-to-day employee services such as cleaning, security, snow removal, lawn mowing, food services, and others.

Sourcing: Act of buying products or services.

Spending Tree: Visualization of spending for subcommodities associated with a commodity or finished product.

Stakeholder: A person or organization that has a say in or is impacted by a project. The stakeholders could be internal or external to the company. Internal stakeholders could be other functions, whereas external stakeholders could be suppliers, community, or government organizations.

Standard Cost: A predetermined cost of performing an operation or producing a good or service under normal conditions.

Statement of Work: A document that contains deliverables and timelines for a vendor providing services to a client. The document also includes detailed requirements, pricing, and terms and conditions.

Strategic Planning: A planning process to define an organization's strategy or direction, and then to make decisions on allocating resources to pursue this strategy.

Streamline: To make an organization or process more efficient and effective by employing faster or simpler working methods.

Subassembly: A unit that is part of a bigger finished product but assembled and tested separately. Subassembly makes it easier to assemble and test the finished product, as the focus is on the interaction between subassemblies.

Supplier Management: The activities include buying products or services, contracting, and providing day-to-day oversight of supplier performance.

Supply Chain: Movement of goods and information from the acquisition of raw materials to delivery of finished goods to the end user.

Supply Fluctuation: Change in availability of raw materials due to outside factors such as transportation problems, strikes, etc.

Support Organization: An organization that is not core to the business but helps in smoother operations of the company. A support organization could be facilities, human resources, procurement, or others.

Survey: A statistical technique to identify trends within a general population by using a small sample from the population. Examples are asking people to complete a questionnaire, collecting rock samples from a geographic area, or collecting data on traffic congestion in a city.

Sustainability: Ability to support the output on an ongoing basis. Sustainability usually refers to environmentally responsible efforts so companies and organizations can continue their activity without depleting natural resources. Some companies explain sustainability with three words—reduce, reuse, and recycle.

System Integration: Refers to bringing together subsystems so that the overall system performs as per expectation. Though the phrase is commonly used in information technology, the concept is valid in any engineering effort.

Telemarketing: Unsolicited marketing of goods or services using telephone calls.

Telepresence: A technology that allows a group of people in different locations to feel as if they were present in the same room during a meeting or conference.

Test Market: Experiment in a geographic region or demographic group to gauge the viability of a new product or service before a wide-scale rollout.

Third-Party Logistics Provider, or 3PL: Refers to a supplier who provides integration of different logistic services to a company. A 3PL may provide oversight to various transportation providers, warehouse providers, or contract manufacturers.

Throughput: Refers to a maximum rate of production or output. It provides an estimation of capacity in the supply chain to meet customer demand.

Transaction Processing: In purchasing, transaction processing refers to discrete activities that must be completed for each transaction. It could be cutting purchase orders, receipt of goods in a warehouse, approving invoices, cutting checks, and other activities. Each of these activities has a set of rules and an approval process that have to be followed before they can be completed.

Transit Procedure: Procedures that dictate how products will be transported from one location to another.

Transportation: Act of moving products from one location to another.

Unbox: Thinking creatively, or "outside the box."

Unbundle: Separating services from a group so they can be procured or performed separately.

Upsell: Practice of attempting to sell a higher-value product to the customer.

Utilization: A measure of number of hours worked by an individual when compared to the total number of work hours. The lower utilization could be due to wait time, travel time, and other reasons that are not under control of the individual performing the task.

World Class: Refers to being the best in the world. Companies use third parties such as consulting firms to declare themselves world class based on a particular set of metrics and benchmarks. Unfortunately, being world class is no guarantee of success in the market, as customers may not value those characteristics.

Zero-Based Budgeting: A budgeting process in which all expenses must be justified each year. In traditional budgeting, managers justify only differences versus past years. By contrast, in zero-based budgeting, a new budget must be made every year without reference to the past.

Zero Inventory: Refers to having no or very little inventory in storage. It is impossible to make supply chain work with no inventory. Companies sometimes use third parties to hold inventory or use accounting techniques to show zero inventory in their financial records.

▪ NOTES ▪

1. "2015's Customer Service Hall of Fame," *USA Today*, http://ow.ly/BSvr3059gJi.

2. "7 Customer Service Lessons from Amazon CEO Jeff Bezos," Salesforce.com, http://ow.ly/E4Yo3059gxj.

3. Amazon Prime is a membership program that gives customers free shipping, access to streaming video, music, e-books, and a variety of other Amazon-specific services and deals.

4. "Amazon's Newest Ambition: Competing Directly with UPS and FedEx," *Wall Street Journal*, http://ow.ly/4QDN3059Drp.

5. The Geek Squad provides services in-store, on-site, and over the Internet via remote access, and also provides 24-hour telephone and emergency on-site support.

6. Facility management is part of the real estate department in a company. It includes day-to-day employee services such as food services, janitorial, safety, occupancy planning, move/add/changes and others.

7. "10 Minutes That Changed Southwest Airlines' Future," *CNBC*, http://ow.ly/lMRM305em6r.

8. "Enhanced Aircraft Development and Support," Airbus, http://ow.ly/neIS3059gbx.

9. "The 787's Problems Run Deeper Than Outsourcing," *Harvard Business Review*, http://ow.ly/fKSS3059gWq.

10. "Boeing Shares Fall 7 Percent on Report of SEC Probe," *CNBC*, http://ow.ly/t5f43059fQy.

11. Cycle time measures time required for a product to reach from one point in supply chain to another.

12. Number of products produced in one single run at a factory.

13. "Starbucks at 40: Java Juggernaut Branches Out," USATODAY.com, http://ow.ly/lcc23059fAf.

14. "Green Juice Featured in the Guardian," http://ow.ly/SPUY3059a0B.

15. "Why Strategic Alliances Fail: New CMO Council Report," *Forbes*, http://ow.ly/9gtg30599Rx.

16. "Steve Jobs on 'Think Different,'" YouTube, http://ow.ly/EINw30599EH.

17. Tim Cook, Wikipedia, https://en.wikipedia.org/wiki/Tim_Cook.

18. U.S. GAO, "Defense Inventory: Actions Needed to Improve the Defense Logistics Agency's Inventory Movement," http://www.gao.gov/products/GAO-14-495.

19. Defense Logistics Agency, or DLA, part of U.S. Department of Defense, manages supplies other than ammunition and weapon systems. It's the largest logistics outfit in the world—estimated to be 10 times the size of Walmart.

20. "Why Most Product Launches Fail," *Harvard Business Review*, https://hbr.org/2011/04/why-most-product-launches-fail.

21. "Boeing's Nuts-and-Bolts Problem," *Wall Street Journal*, http://ow.ly/dzEL305em1s.

22. Market research, Wikipedia, http://ow.ly/yX7S305991Z.

23. An outsourcing provider that provides services across diverse areas such as project management, landscaping, construction, janitorial, food services, and energy management.

24. "Vested Outsourcing: How P&G Brought Its Focus on Innovation to Facilities Management," Area Development, http://ow.ly/2o0r30598VH.

25. GMP, guaranteed maximum price—the contractor is compensated for actual costs incurred plus a fixed fee subject to a ceiling price.

26. Removing an agent between supplier and customers.

27. "AT&T's Cingular Success Story," Bloomberg, http://ow.ly/JPIC30598HJ.

INDEX

Printed in the USA
CPSIA information can be obtained
at www.ICGtesting.com
LVHW031522120823
755048LV00006B/42